"This book will help you become a  effectively deal with parenting situat of your own values, thoughts, and fee let go of the past, and take your ch the future."

—Thomas J. Dishion, Ph.D., codirector of the Child and Family Center, professor of psychology at the University of Oregon

"Acceptance and commitment therapy (ACT) is one of the newest, most influential, and most powerful forms of therapy to be developed by psychologists in a long, long time. As scientific support for ACT grows, so too has the breadth of its application. This book is an example of a new frontier for that growth—parenting. By reading and carefully following the advice this book contains, you can not only become a more effective parent, but also a more effective and happier person."

—Patrick C. Friman, Ph.D., ABPP, director of clinical services at Boys Town, clinical professor of pediatrics at University of Nebraska School of Medicine

"For many, the joys of parenting are lost, hidden by the mind's chatter to 'parent the right way' or by the heart's desire to escape the emotional pitfalls of parenting. But the joys of parenting are found in the space that lies between parent and child—in a relationship where parents know the value of simply being with their child. Lisa Coyne and Amy Murrell wisely and gently guide readers to that space."

—Timothy A. Cavell, Ph.D., author of *Working with Parents of Aggressive Children* and *You're Not the Worst Parent in the World*

"Parenting is always challenging, no matter how much we love our children. This book offers practical ways to accept the challenge, choose what matters most in our relationship with our children, and take action to build this relationship one day at a time."

—Jean E. Dumas, Ph.D.

"Most people know that parenting is a supremely difficult job and no one ever gets it right all the time. This book is filled with examples, questions, exercises, and strategies to help you look at who you are as a parent: your values, your limits, and your fears, and thus enable you to do what's right (for you and your child), not what's easy."

—Carolyn Boehne, LICSW

"I was at the end of my rope with my daughter. I called around and was able to find this program, ACT, and it was very helpful. I had hope that things would work out when they gave me ways to deal with the issues at home. My daughter is doing great, and I think it's because of some of the things I was able to use from the ACT program."

—Liz S., client

"ACT taught me that there isn't a perfect or easy fix to my problems, but I learned not to get so wrapped up in my child's behavior. I am calmer in most situations now, and that facilitates my understanding of myself as well as my child."

—Traci S., client

the joy of parenting

parenting

an acceptance & commitment therapy guide
to effective parenting in the early years

Lisa W. Coyne, Ph.D.
Amy R. Murrell, Ph.D.

New Harbinger Publications, Inc.

Publisher's Note

This publication is designed to provide accurate and authoritative information in regard to the subject matter covered. It is sold with the understanding that the publisher is not engaged in rendering psychological, financial, legal, or other professional services. If expert assistance or counseling is needed, the services of a competent professional should be sought.

Distributed in Canada by Raincoast Books

Copyright © 2009 by Lisa W. Coyne & Amy R. Murrell
New Harbinger Publications, Inc.
5674 Shattuck Avenue
Oakland, CA 94609
www.newharbinger.com

Acquired by Tesilya Hanauer; Cover design by Amy Shoup;
Edited by Jean M. Blomquist; Text design by Tracy Marie Carlson

Library of Congress Cataloging-in-Publication Data

Coyne, Lisa W.
  The joy of parenting : an acceptance and commitment therapy guide to effective parent
ing in the early years / Lisa W. Coyne and Amy R. Murrell ; foreword by Kelly Wilson.
    p. cm.
  Includes bibliographical references.
  ISBN-13: 978-1-57224-593-8 (pbk. : alk. paper)
  ISBN-10: 1-57224-593-X (alk. paper)
  1. Parenting. 2. Acceptance and commitment therapy. I. Murrell, Amy R. II. Title.
HQ755.8.C69 2009
649'.64--dc22
                                    2009023486

18   17   16

10   9   8   7   6   5   4

For my children, Josie and Rory. You are my greatest joy.

—LWC

To my own parents, for teaching me that life is perfectly whole.

—ARM

Contents

Dear reader:

Welcome to New Harbinger Publications. New Harbinger is dedicated to publishing books based on acceptance and commitment therapy (ACT) and its application to specific areas. New Harbinger has a long-standing reputation as a publisher of quality, well-researched books for general and professional audiences.

There are many books on parenting based on well-researched behavior management techniques that parents can learn to apply to their own children. The unique strength of this book is that it incorporates all this knowledge in a new context that goes beyond teaching traditional behavior management techniques. For instance, much of the book focuses on how parents can learn to apply behavior management techniques in a much more thoughtful and effective way by incorporating acceptance and mindfulness techniques. It also uses and brings to life ACT principles that provide you with an understanding of how your child's mind—just like your own—is often playing tricks on your child and yourself. It provides you with fun techniques to teach your kids and yourself to recognize when your mind may not be your best friend and to relate differently to your critical mind by learning to simply observe your mind and focus on the important and cool stuff that really matters in life.

The book does not lecture you or make prescriptions, and the authors present information in a very accessible and easy-to-read style. It is written with compassion and from an understanding of how difficult parenting often is in our increasingly more complex world. The book helps you identify, clarify, and then stick with your own parenting values and goals. Being aware and in tune with those values is particularly important and helpful when you encounter truly challenging and difficult issues with your kids. The authors encourage and show you how you can confront those issues without becoming overwhelmed by them and how to take care of yourself when you feel stressed out because things are not working out as planned.

The book provides many useful case examples and lots of concrete exercises and practical suggestions which will help you adapt the methods described to the particular situation you find yourself in with your kids. Although the book provides information that is applicable to many different parenting situations and everyday life problems, it also makes specific suggestions for some common problems of childhood such as those that involve anxiety and acting out (e.g., tantrums, aggression).

As part of New Harbinger's commitment to publishing books based on sound, scientific, clinical research, we oversee all prospective books for the Acceptance and Commitment Therapy Series. Serving as series editors, we comment on proposals and offer guidance as needed, and use a gentle hand in making suggestions regarding the content, depth, and scope of each book.

Books in the Acceptance and Commitment Therapy Series:

- Have an adequate database, appropriate to the strength of the claims being made.

- Are theoretically coherent. They will fit with the ACT model and underlying behavioral principles as they have evolved at the time of writing.

- Orient the reader toward unresolved empirical issues.

- Do not overlap needlessly with existing volumes.

- Avoid jargon and unnecessary entanglement with proprietary methods, leaving ACT work open and available.

- Keep the focus always on what is good for the reader.

- Support the further development of the field.

- Provide information in a way that is of practical use to readers.

These guidelines reflect the values of the broader ACT community. You'll see all of them packed into this book.

Sincerely,

Georg H. Eifert, Ph.D.,
John P. Forsyth, Ph.D.,
Steven C. Hayes, Ph.D., and
Robyn Walser, Ph.D.

Foreword

In the fall of 2000, I began my faculty post at the University of Mississippi—Ole Miss to those who love her. Amy Murrell was one of my first students. Lisa Coyne, a student of my colleague Alan Gross, soon joined the Acceptance and Commitment Therapy (ACT) Treatment Development Group. At that time, there had been virtually no ACT work done with children. My training had been focused mainly on adults, and we were only treating adults in my lab. Amy and Lisa chastised me for my reluctance to treat or supervise the treatment of children.

"Do we have to wait until two decades have beat them up before we treat them?!" they protested.

It made sense to me that ACT principles could be applied to children as well as to adults, and I couldn't think of a sound reason our little group shouldn't explore this application. And though I probably resisted the idea longer than I should have, Amy and Lisa finally compelled me by dint of sound argument and dogged persistence to work with children. I saw children, they saw children, and together, we found our way. Together, we sorted out ways to give ACT a voice that could be heard by children. Someone had to do that work, and looking back, I've glad that we saw the opportunity and took it.

When I read this volume, I heard that voice we found together years ago, now refined and amplified by the years of experience shared by these authors, both of whom are exceptional scholars and clinicians. And though that voice speaks softly to children, the book itself is written to adults, to parents in particular. When you work with children, you work with parents—or at least you hope to work with parents. Why? Not because parents are the cause of children's problems. Rather, because in their parents' care is where children learn and grow the most.

As we all are, some children are born to wealth and some to poverty. Circumstance may dictate how much time we can spend caring for our children. But even under the most challenging of circumstances, it's possible to bring love and kindness to our interactions with them—even though we may not always feel loving and kind. For those parents who choose to make a commitment to creating a kind, loving, and nurturing space for their children, this book shows the way.

Lisa and Amy provide practical ways to help us take time, even in the busiest schedule, to see, feel, and appreciate our children. There's a way in which openness and acceptance can alter our sense of time, where each moment we get with our children is sufficient unto itself. My own youngest children are near grown now. The years go by so quickly. I would ask you, the reader, to use this book to make the most of the time you have with your children. I know that this is what Amy and Lisa care about, this is why they pushed our little group at Ole Miss to pursue this work, this is why they took the time to write this book.

If I could offer a word of advice, it would be this. Be patient. Take your time. Work through the exercises, and let the exercises do their work. See if in doing so you begin to regard your children as a bit more precious—and so, too, the time you spend with them. Our children don't come with an instruction manual, but sometimes a little instruction can be a help.

—Kelly G. Wilson, Ph.D.
Madrid, Spain
June, 2009

Acknowledgments

Together we would like to thank the ACT community for being committed to developing a science that matters for people. We would also like to say thank you to the New Harbinger staff, particularly Tesilya Hanauer and Jess Beebe, and to our copy editor, Jean Blomquist. Finally, we would like to express our greatest gratitude to the many families who helped this book come to life: to all of the children who have allowed us to learn about parenting and to all of the parents who have shared their struggles and joys with us. Your stories and courage inspire us beyond words. We hope that this book is of use to you.

—LC & AM

Many people helped in the shaping and writing of this book. To Alan Gross and Kelly Wilson, thank you for your mentorship and support through the years. To Henrietta Leonard, Jennifer Freeman, Abbe Garcia, and Lynda Field, thank you for your friendship and guidance. To the members of the Early Childhood Research Clinic, thank you for your helpful thoughts, your excellent work, and your patience throughout this process. For Mei Hua Fu, Regina Wong, Pat Landry, Carolyn Boehne, and all the teachers at the Chinese Church and Native American Head Start programs in Boston, thank you for working with us, for your many talents, and for your incredible commitment to the young children and families you serve. To my incredible colleagues Amy Marks, David Pantalone, Elisabeth Sandberg, Gary Fireman, Sue Orsillo, and Lance Swenson, thank you for your humor, your support, and your open office doors. Finally, to my husband, John, I owe you my deepest love and gratitude for going through this process with me—and deciding to stay.

—Lisa W. Coyne, Ph.D.

In addition to the extraordinary families who helped shape this work, a number of people deserve mention for my place in it. This book would not have been possible if not for my mentor, Kelly Wilson, and the amazing students with whom I have the pleasure of sharing what he taught me. I am forever grateful. I also thank my colleagues who encouraged and supported me throughout the process. When others advised me not to write a book at this point in my career, they stood by me—and reminded me what I really care about. And, to my husband, Roy—thank you for being supportive of my valuing, and for understanding long days and nights at the computer.

—Amy R. Murrell, Ph.D.

CHAPTER 1

An ACT Philosophy of Parenting

Accept, Choose, and Take Action

If the day ever came when we were able to accept ourselves and our children exactly as we are and they are, then, I believe we would have come to an understanding of what "good parenting" means.

Fred Rogers

We all have dreams for our children. We want them to grow up happy and safe. When they leave our arms, we want them to find relationships with others who love and cherish them as we do. We want them to be successful and independent, compassionate and wise. We also want to play a role in ensuring that these dreams come true. This is especially meaningful during the toddler and preschool years. During these years, we as parents are the world for our children—there will never be another developmental period in which our children depend on us so completely. This is the time when we are best able to shape their experiences so that they might attain their own dreams. However, as we all know well, this is easier said than done. Sometimes when we are most unsure or when our children are most challenging, our minds kick in and begin their commentary. We evaluate our actions as parents, our choices in the moment, and the behavior of our children.

Have you, for example, ever worried that your two-year-old's rages might herald conduct problems that would derail his learning? Or that your four-year-old's clinginess and separation fears might signify more intense anxieties or overdependence on others? Or that the parenting strategies you're using might contribute to your child's problems down the road? At the same time, how do you know when behavior problems *really* mean that problems lie ahead? When should you step in? How?

If you're human, your mind has probably whispered these worries to you, especially when you're feeling stressed or vulnerable. No matter what's happening with our children, our minds give us plenty to worry about. And, almost as if without choice, we listen to what our minds say. Sometimes we listen so hard that it becomes impossible to hear anything else. And in those moments, we may actually be at risk for problems in how we behave toward our children—and how they behave toward us. Parenting is a difficult task, and we're often our own worst critics. Sometimes that makes the task of parenting all the more difficult.

You Are Not Alone in Your Struggles as a Parent

Think about your darkest moments as a parent—those of which you are least proud or that you would want to erase, if that were possible. Imagine that you're sitting with a therapist who has just asked you to describe them. How much of these experiences would you feel comfortable sharing? How much would you keep to yourself? You might be surprised to hear that, without exception, all of the parents who come to us for help feel ashamed or embarrassed about their feelings about or reactions to their children. It's as though there's an invisible censor in their heads that says, *Oh no, don't say that,* or *Good parents would never think those things,* or *She'll think I'm an idiot if I say that.* Here are some examples of what parents begin to share, when they feel ready:

- "I wish I could just take a vacation and be left alone. I'm so overwhelmed by being needed all the time."

- "Every time she misbehaves at the mall, I feel like I just want to run away."

- "My kids exhaust me. I never asked for this. I had no idea it would be like this."

- "I get so angry with him that I feel like I'm going to lose control."

What's it like for you to read these parents' experiences? Is your first impulse to think, "Oh no, that's not me." Or somewhere, on some level, do you identify with such thoughts even in a small way? Parents have learned from other parents, and from society as a whole, to hide thoughts and feelings like this. We're taught that they are wrong and bad. Even to read them may elicit thoughts about parents who might "lose it" and harm their children. To admit to having feelings like this is culturally equated with "bad parenting." You might feel some relief in knowing that other parents feel this way too, but that relief probably doesn't last long when you're looking around at other parents who seem to have it all put together. Think about how television, movies, and parenting magazines depict mothers and, to a lesser extent, fathers. The media tends to portray parents as perfect, always available to their children, always happy, and in control. When you see such images, your mind might engage in social comparisons in which you almost always come up short.

That's not the whole story, however: your mind can also be critical of other parents. Have you ever negatively judged other parents when you see their children misbehave at the playground, in a restaurant, or at a mall? Your head spins with ideas about what "those parents" are doing wrong and what they could do right. But here's the catch: imagine yourself in a similar situation—your child acts out and you notice other parents observing you. Based on what we hear from our clients, and what we've experienced ourselves, our guess is that your mind is no less harsh toward your own perceived flaws, fumbles, and foibles as a parent. Many parents feel that their children's misbehavior is a sign of their own failures. And, like it or not, those feelings are a normal part of the parenting experience. Certainly these things are difficult to acknowledge. And as clinicians, we're hard-pressed to think of a parent who hasn't experienced some variation of these thoughts and feelings. Not surprisingly, most parents respond to thinking and feeling like this by attempting to hide it from others and from themselves. Unfortunately, although this strategy might seem useful in the moment, it may have devastating consequences in the long run. One of the most important of these unintended negative consequences is that parents feel alone, as though they're the only ones who've ever had "bad" thoughts and feelings like these.

This book will show you that you're not alone. It's for and about parents of young children, and it will speak to your experiences of parenting. It will provide meaningful options for coping with difficult thoughts and feelings in the face of common behavioral changes and challenges presented by early childhood. We'll help you learn how to step out of your own mind and practice being with, seeing, and experiencing your child for the incredible, beautiful, and vulnerable being that she is—when she is at her best and, more importantly, at her worst. We'll teach you how to mindfully, compassionately parent your young child, even in his, or your, most difficult or vulnerable moments.

An Acceptance and Commitment Therapy (ACT) Model of Parenting

Acceptance and commitment therapy (ACT) is a therapeutic approach that emphasizes compassionate acknowledgment and acceptance of our own experiences, in the service of effectively pursuing those things in life that matter most to us. This chapter will introduce ACT as a philosophy of living and encourage you as a parent, through experiential exercises, to explore and identify how ACT describes your own experiences with your child. From an ACT-based perspective, we believe that how you approach your thoughts and feelings, especially in the context of your relationships with your child, is a key ingredient of effective parenting. Your values and vulnerabilities serve as lenses through which you view your child and focus your choices in how to nurture him, provide guidance, and set limits. ACT-based parenting will help you compassionately acknowledge and accept your feelings, worries, or perceived inadequacies. In the most challenging moments, the goal is to notice and accept your feelings and thoughts as they are, without attempting to change them, so that you may appreciate your child in the moment and stand up for what matters most—for what's most meaningful in your relationship with your young child.

Parenting During the Early Childhood Years

Having good relationships and setting appropriate limits with your child is important at all developmental stages, and it's especially important in early childhood.

The early childhood years (from age two through age eight) herald many changes, transitions, and challenges for families. Although this developmental period may seem brief, it holds an incredibly diverse set of milestones both for your child and for you. Just as your child grows up and changes, so do you as a parent. One can think of parenting during the early childhood years as a parallel period of development. Just as your child advances in social, emotional, and behavioral sophistication, your parenting strategies necessarily develop and change. Sometimes these processes go hand in hand. Other times, however, they may seem to be at odds.

Early childhood is a time when you must sensitively guide, and at the same time, firmly set limits with your child. Sometimes it isn't possible for you to take a break or get a breather, as your young child needs a lot of different things. It's often a difficult balancing act. It's hard to know how much guidance to give and how much to allow your child to make her own discoveries. Similarly it's sometimes confusing to figure out when to set limits and when to relax them. Moreover, as your child develops and grows to be a more sophisticated thinker and more perceptive social being, you must be ready to change your strategies to match these changes in development.

Transitions in Your Parenting

Although all parents change and grow to keep pace with their children's cognitive, emotional, and behavioral development, sometimes these parenting transitions are painfully difficult. Think about your own experience. These transitions may come, for example, at a time when you are feeling your most vulnerable and overwhelmed. Just as you establish one routine, you may find that you need to shift to another. As your young child grows, he seeks more autonomy, hungers for more knowledge, and moves from utter dependence on his family to become more involved in relationships with his friends at school. However, knowing that these transitions are normal doesn't necessarily make them any easier. In fact, it may make things even harder because as your child ages, you may feel as though his behavior is less and less under your control.

Traditional Behavioral Approaches to Parenting

There are many effective parent training programs that emphasize helping parents change their children's behavior, in part through changing their own parenting tactics. Most of these approaches address parenting difficulties as a "skills deficit"—that is, they carry the assumption that parents lack the skills to effectively change their children's behavior. Thus, they strive to teach new parenting skills, such as how to effectively build (or rebuild) relationships with your child, how to set limits consistently, or how to ensure that your child follows directions.

Most models of behavioral parent training that treat aggression and noncompliance (that is, when your child doesn't do what you ask her to do) are based on the work of the social learning scientist Gerald Patterson (1982), who has conducted extensive research on children and families over the past few decades. Generally speaking, behavioral problems tend to occur most often in families when parents do three things:

1. Fail to notice when children behave well.

2. Pay too much attention to negative behaviors.

3. Make empty threats or escalating demands on children.

These three parenting actions tend to maintain child behavior problems such as noncompliance, tantrums, and aggression. In short, children may misbehave partly in response to your escalating threats combined with difficulty following through.

Likewise your child may learn to coerce you into giving in instead of sticking to developmentally appropriate demands. To use a classic example, think of a mother and child in the checkout line at the grocery store. The child begs, softly at first, to get some candy. The mother says no and asks the child to be quiet. The child raises his voice and begins to cry. The mother still says no, and the child's behavior gets worse. The mother gets embarrassed. Her heart rate goes up, she begins to sweat, and, as people begin to stare, she thinks a lot about her failure as a parent. All too often, the mother gives in and buys the child some candy. Thus, most research-based models of parenting teach how to pay attention to and reward "good" behavior, how to wisely choose what misbehaviors can be ignored, and how to give directions simply and effectively. These approaches are usually taught in the context of improving the parent–child relationship, which may need repair.

The Missing Link: The Parent's Thoughts and Feelings

While sound knowledge and skillful use of these techniques are extremely important, this is only part of the whole picture of what sometimes makes child rearing difficult for parents. It is known that the single most important reason why proven behavioral approaches to parenting sometimes don't work is that parents use them inconsistently or incorrectly. But what exactly are the obstacles that get in the way of using these techniques?

Certainly some children are more difficult to parent than others. For example, some children resist separation or seem more anxious than others. Some may be more oppositional (that is, stubborn and argumentative) or might not respond well to rewards. Others might be picky eaters, or resist bedtime, or struggle with getting along with other children. Even though the vast majority of these issues reflect variability in normal development, if they are happening to your child, you may feel at a loss for what to do or how to think through the problems. However, this doesn't fully complete the picture either. Why are some parents able to effectively parent difficult children, or even typical children, during challenging developmental transitions? Why do some parents struggle despite their children being well behaved and progressing normally on their developmental trajectories? Why is it that even when parents are doing a wonderful job, they may be self-critical and focus on perceived failures instead of successes, or on what their children lack instead of what they have?

Most approaches to child behavior have little appreciation for what's going on in your head as you raise your young child. This aspect of parenting is left largely untouched and untapped in the empirical literature on effective behavioral parenting techniques. Although there are many excellent behavioral parent training programs that import principles shown to be effective with young children through elegant clinical trials, there is far less information on how and when to use these techniques when parents feel overwhelmed or have difficulty implementing them. How you as parent behave and interact with your child depends on the particular situation at hand. Part of what makes certain situations or contexts so difficult to handle are your thoughts and feelings about them, and the meanings that you give to them. Consider the following examples:

- Janine is the mother of four-year-old Rex. She values being a loving mother and attempts to help Rex stay at an even keel. She believes if he gets upset, it reflects poorly on her ability to help him learn to handle his emotions, and it means that she is not a competent parent. Thus, when Rex demands things such as toys at the store or special snacks, she usually gives in. Sometimes she tries to resist in order to teach him that he can't always get what he wants, but he screams and stomps his feet, so she feels that she has no choice other than to let him have what he wants. However, his behavior has become a problem as the family is on a tight budget and Janine has been overspending to satisfy Rex's demands for toys and special treats.

- MaKaya is the single mother of a six-year-old boy, Armand, and twin girls, Keisha and Angela, who are two and a half years. She often feels that the twins demand most of her time, and she relies on Armand to help out and to do quickly what he is told. However, since starting kindergarten, he doesn't seem to follow directions quickly. When MaKaya has to ask repeatedly for him to do things, like pick up his toys or run and get a diaper for one of the twins, she feels her irritation rising. She raises her voice and yells at him for not following directions. Sometimes she threatens him with spanking, and sometimes she just gives up. Sometimes he screams back at her. Lately she feels helpless and overwhelmed. Every time he looks at her a certain way, it's as though there's a little voice in her head that tells her she's failing him, that she isn't doing enough to help him grow into a responsible adult. She avoids Armand when she can by telling him to go play in his room.

■ Peter is the father of five-year-old Sarah. Peter learned that when a child breaks a rule, the child should be punished. So when Sarah breaks a rule, he has her sit on the bottom step of the staircase as a time-out. One day, while Peter was working on his computer, Sarah came to him to tell him something that happened at school. Because she broke the rule for not interrupting him when he's working, he sent her to time-out. She seemed more upset than usual and came back to speak to him two more times. He believed in the rules, however, and wanted her to learn to comply without exception. So he continued putting her in time-out and finally sent her to bed without reading a story or tucking under the covers. The next morning his wife told him Sarah had simply wanted to talk about a fight with a friend at school that had made her very sad. He felt angry with his wife for making him feel guilty, and he felt regretful that he had missed the opportunity to support and grow closer to his daughter. He wondered if he had made the right choice.

For each of these parents, thoughts and feelings have gotten in the way of really *seeing* and responding in sensitive ways to their children. Your mind, just like the minds of these parents, may criticize you when you don't parent effectively, and that can make things worse. The good news is that you can choose to mind—or be mindful of—your child instead of minding your mind.

Minding Your Child, or Minding Your Mind?

We all have pressures that are put on us by ourselves as well as by others. As a parent, you must balance child rearing with the many other demands of your busy life, including your own stressors, emotions, and self-evaluations. You may not realize it, but you're always evaluating yourself, your parenting, and your child. To get a better understanding of this, we invite you to take a look at your process of self-evaluation in the exercise below. Get a notebook you can use as a "parenting journal" in which you can write your answers. (You'll need the parenting journal for exercises throughout this book.)

EXERCISE: Noticing Your Mind

Think of the last time when you were with your child when he wasn't behaving well and other parents were present. Try to remember as many details about that situation as you can; picture it as if you're watching a scene in a movie, then place yourself in that scene. While there, reflect on the questions below. Write your answers in your parenting journal.

- Where are you? What's happening? How does your child misbehave? What do you do? What is your face like? How about your body language?

- What is it like to experience your child misbehaving in front of an audience? Do you question how you handled (or didn't handle) the situation? Does a thought flash across your mind about what the other parents might think or how you look to them while interacting with your child? Do you change your behavior to make it more acceptable to the other parents or even to your child? Do you get hooked by your thoughts and try to push them away, talk yourself out of them, or question their logic?

- Does your attention shift out of the moment, as your mind goes into overdrive, presenting options for what you should do next or how you can avoid the consequences you feared?

After you've reflected on these questions, come back to the present moment. Note whether it's easy or somewhat awkward to pick up where you left off in this book. If it's hard to pick up where you left off, is that because you're so wrapped up in remembering the experience of your child misbehaving in public?

If you've ever experienced thinking like this—felt unsure of yourself or noticed yourself looking at your actions as though through the eyes of a harsh critic—welcome to being human. You are human, and you have a fine, critical mind. Think of it this way: Your mind is a wonderful ally in many, many situations. It helps you plan for the future and evaluate courses of action to pick the best ones for yourself, your child, your family. Your mind helps you evaluate unseen dangers and contributes to how you structure your days and your time with your children. Your mind allows you to contemplate the future without having experienced it, and it allows you to reminisce about and learn from the past. Minds work the same way for everyone and bind us together as humans. Unfortunately, for all the advantages they give us, minds also sometimes get in the way of our interactions with our children and blind us to the present moment.

If this "blinding" is familiar to you, again, welcome to being human. You were "minding your mind," something we all do. And since you're human, you haven't discovered an "off" switch for your mind, except maybe for very short intervals. That's because there really isn't an off switch: minds do what minds do. Your mind is the critic you hear every day, sometimes every moment. Your mind is always talking to you, evaluating your actions, and scolding you for doing things wrong, for feeling too much or too little, or for "losing it" with your children. Why? The purpose of your mind is to protect you from harm, whether real or perceived. Sometimes, however, your mind is a bit overzealous. And when you focus entirely on wrestling with your mind, you may parent "automatically" without noticing what's really going on in the moment with your child. Here's a story, told to us by a mother named Linda, that will illustrate what we mean.

❧ Paying Attention to the Moment

One morning my five-year old daughter put lipstick on before kindergarten, even though she knew it wasn't permitted. We were running late, my frustration level was already high, and my head was full of unpleasant thoughts—that my daughter had willfully broken a rule and attempted to sneak the lipstick past me, that the teachers and other parents would think that I was an inattentive parent if my child went to school with lipstick on, that the extra time needed to convince my child to take off the lipstick would make me late for the train and thus my job, that I would be reprimanded for my tardiness, and that would be terrible, and so on. I could feel my level of irritation rising like mercury in a thermometer, and I started to yell at my daughter. I meant not only for her to get the lipstick off but also for her to know how angry I was as well as the consequences of her action for both of us. I went on and on until my little girl's eyes grew shiny with tears and she said, "But Mommy, I feel so little—and lipstick makes me feel big."

Linda told us that her daughter had always been the physically smallest child in her class. Because of her size, she endured teachers' low expectations, peers who expected her to always be the "baby" when they played house, and, at worst, verbal and physical bullying. "And yet," Linda said to us, "there I was, trying to cut my child down to size. Because I was busy wrestling with the weight of all my own negative thoughts, I missed what was really going on in that moment for my child. My little girl was feeling her littleness and looking for a way to be strong in a world where most everyone was bigger than her. Although on the face of it, setting a limit seemed to me the right thing to do, I'd missed the bigger—and much more important—picture. I reacted to my *thoughts* instead of being responsive to my child's *needs*. This particular moment could have been a time where we might have connected. I missed an opportunity to know and understand my child's experience and to draw closer to her."

How Mindfulness Changes Parenting

All parents feel overwhelmed at times. When we experience self-critical or self-evaluative thoughts like the ones Linda experienced in the preceding story, we become "stuck" in our minds. When we're stuck, we pay attention to our minds and lose track of what's going on with our children. In these situations, we believe "mindfulness" is a helpful skill for parents—and particularly for parents of young children, like you. So what exactly is "mindfulness"? *Mindfulness* is a compassionate, rich, and nondefensive awareness of the present moment. It takes a good deal of practice, but when cultivated over time, mindfulness can help you experience moments—even difficult ones—with your child more fully so that you can parent more thoughtfully and effectively.

Recent research by professor of psychiatry and pediatrics Nirbhay Singh and colleagues (2007) suggests that attending to your thoughts, feelings, and experiences of parenting is critical to effectively nurturing and setting appropriate limits with children. When you get "stuck" in the management and control of your thoughts and feelings, your full attention is drawn away from your child. However, if you can simply acknowledge what you're thinking and feeling without responding to it, you may attend more fully to your child and thus may be able to parent in more sensitive, responsive ways.

For example, *supportive parenting* refers to understanding, acknowledging, and acting in ways that support your child's intentions and goals. Supportive parenting may be especially important in early childhood. As a supportive parent, you help show your child appropriate ways to get what he wants. You collaborate with your child as a more sophisticated "partner" and help him to remain focused and to see activities through. Here's an example of supportive parenting: A young child is working on her first puzzle. She begins to get frustrated and attempts to break some of the puzzle pieces to make them fit in the puzzle board. Her father sits down beside her and gently acknowledges that she's having a hard time. Then, without completing the puzzle for his daughter, the father talks to the girl and teaches her several options (for example, matching the outlines, turning pieces around). He also talks to her about her feelings and asks if she wants help. This father helps his daughter to reach her goal: completing the puzzle. He does this through noticing—but not trying to change or control—her emotions. Attending to children's goals helps parents to create a supportive environment that helps their children master developmental skills they need in order to take on other challenges as they grow up.

A recent study by parenting researcher Theodore Dix and his colleagues (2004) has shown that when parents focus on their young children's motives and intentions in the moment rather than their own thoughts and feelings, they're more likely to engage in behaviors that support their children's goals. In this study, for example, when parents were more depressed, they reported fewer child-focused and more parent-focused emotions; they behaved in ways less likely to support their children. When parents felt negative emotions such as anger, they were also less in tune with their children (Dix et al. 2004). This suggests that parents engaged in efforts to change their own emotions are less likely to be focused on and sensitive to their children's needs.

Trying to avoid or suppress unwanted thoughts or feelings—what we call *experiential avoidance*—may lead to ineffective parenting. Why? Because when you try to avoid your thoughts and feelings, you tend to

■ use rigid and inflexible parenting strategies;

■ be inconsistent with your use of parenting tactics, such as saying no and then going back on it and saying yes;

■ overreact to your child's negative emotion (anger, anxiety, frustration, and so on);

■ focus on and respond to misbehavior rather than praise your child's good behavior; and

■ pay attention to your mind instead of your child.

There is growing evidence that mindfulness, or mindful awareness, may help you attend to your child's needs, goals, and desires. For example, *empathic awareness*—the ability to predict your child's motives and desires or to imagine his thoughts and feelings—is closely linked with mindfulness. Mindfulness also makes it more likely that you can learn and accommodate new information about your child that might be inconsistent with your previous experiences with him. All children change and grow; if you are mindfully aware of your child, you will likely notice these changes quickly and be able to respond more effectively to them. Parents with empathic awareness report that their children have fewer behavioral difficulties, and these parents report being happier themselves (Coyne et al. 2006). A few studies have shown that parents who are less accepting of their own experiences are more likely to experience stress as a parent (for example, Blackledge and Hayes 2006). And conversely, as parents work on being mindful and accepting of their children and their own parenting abilities, they become better parents and their children tend to have fewer behavioral problems (Oppenheim, Goldsmith, and Koren-Karie 2004). This suggests that mindful awareness and acceptance of our children, of our relationships with them, and of ourselves as parents and people will help us to experience parenting more fully and to be responsive, rather than simply reactive, parents.

On Experiential Avoidance

As we mentioned above, experiential avoidance—the tendency to avoid or suppress unwanted thoughts or feelings—is related to parental stress (Blackledge and Hayes 2006). One recent study has also suggested that attempts to avoid unwanted thoughts and feelings about parenting make it harder to learn new tasks or implement learned skills (Murrell et al., in press). That may be because when you work hard on controlling what you think and feel, your attention is taken away from the task at hand. For example, imagine you're playing tennis but are also required to be doing "serial 7s," or counting upward in groups of seven, as you play. Even though the two tasks are totally unrelated, no doubt your tennis performance would decline. Likewise, if you're trying to help your child deal with a frustrating task that's slightly beyond her ability, you'll find that helping her will be even more difficult if you're also trying to stop your mind from making critical comments about your performance. It's like parenting while doing serial 7s.

Stop Struggling with Your Thoughts and Feelings

A bit earlier, we discussed thoughts and feelings many parents have shared with us about difficult situations or interactions with their children. Most parents struggle with these thoughts. You may try to ignore them, change them through logical arguments, or distract yourself from your thoughts. If particular strategies don't work fast enough, you might try different ones that work even less well. You almost certainly keep your thoughts and feelings to yourself. All these strategies have a common thread: they all constitute unwillingness to acknowledge and accept your own experiences; that is, they're a form of experiential avoidance. We'll expand on this idea in future chapters and show you how attempts to control how you think and feel interfere with effective parenting.

Have you ever been worried about something and continued wrestling with it or had trouble getting it out of your mind? Maybe it kept you from focusing on activities during the day or prevented you from getting to sleep at night. Maybe it started taking up more and more of your mental space, occupying a larger proportion of your thoughts. As a result, you may have felt increasingly tired, less hopeful, or more tense.

This kind of experience is like struggling in quicksand. Naturally you want to get away from your worries, yet struggling to push them away only draws you deeper and deeper in, making it harder and harder to escape. But there's another option. It may seem farfetched, and it may even seem like the opposite of what you should do. But sometimes, just as if you're trapped in quicksand, the best thing to do is stop struggling and stay still. If you become still, you'll stop sinking. You might notice available means of getting out of the quicksand that you hadn't seen before. Sometimes stepping out of a struggle is the most effective thing to do.

But, you might ask, "What does this have to do with what I'm thinking and feeling?" Well, think about all the thoughts and feelings you have about your parenting, your child, or yourself. Being surrounded by them is like being in quicksand, and the more you struggle, the more disheartened you might become or the less focused on moment-to-moment interactions with your child. Those thoughts and feelings may also become more and more intense or frequent until they compose the fabric of your life and of your relationship with your child. See if this fits with your experience: when you're with your child in difficult moments, does it seem that these negative thoughts grow more intense or become more persistent?

In this book, we'll show you that trying to control your thoughts and feelings—or those of your child—is a compelling but futile exercise. By learning to simply and compassionately notice and accept your thoughts and feelings rather than fighting them, you'll learn to bring your full mindful awareness to your relationship with your child. What would it be like to turn to your child and actually see him and appreciate him even in his worst moments? What would it be like to learn to be gentle with yourself as a parent and to understand that all of us humans, whether parents or not, are engaged in the same struggle with our thoughts and feelings?

Accept, Choose, and Take Action

Acceptance and commitment therapy (ACT) helps you notice your thoughts and feelings without being controlled by them. It helps you to act on your values concerning your children rather than to react to what your mind tells you. (We'll talk more about your parenting values in chapter 3.) You can easily remember the components of an ACT-based approach to parenting by simply thinking A-C-T: accept (A), choose (C), take action (T). We'll show you in more detail how to do this in the chapters that follow. For now, here are the basics.

Accept

One of the first and most important things that ACT-based parenting will teach you is how to accept your thoughts, feelings, and experiences with compassion. We'll discuss the ways in which your emotions, thoughts, beliefs, negative self-evaluations, and social comparisons as a parent show up when you strive to meet the daily demands placed on you by your child and by your role as a caregiver. Accepting and being aware of such experiences rather than engaging in a struggle to manage them will pave the way to richer, more mindful interactions with your child.

Choose

In the beginning of this chapter, we talked about dreams—for your child, for your family, and for yourself as a parent. The "choose" component of ACT will help you identify and realize the things that matter most to you as a parent and for your relationship with your young child. It will help you "live out" your family relationships and parenting values. As part of "choosing" what type of parent you want to be, take a few moments with the exercise below. Be sure to write your thoughts in your journal.

EXERCISE: What Type of Parent Do You Want to Be?

Close your eyes and take a couple of deep breaths. Consider the following questions:

- What type of parent do you want to be?

- What kind of world would make it possible for you to change or deepen your relationship with your young child to nurture her development, goals, and intentions?

The choosing component of ACT helps you work *for* what means most to you rather than *against* what you most fear.

Take Action

The final component of ACT—take action—encourages you to make a commitment to pursue your most cherished values with integrity, even in the face of great difficulty and stress. You'll learn how to behave in ways that are consistent with the things that you value the most. You'll also learn that you as a person are much more than the sum total of your thoughts. You'll explore those things that get in the way of living out your values in your relationships with your child. Most concretely, you'll learn effective behavior management strategies. The taking-action component of ACT is about saying yes to what matters most to you as a parent, and meaning that yes with your whole heart.

The Mind Returns

A moment ago, as you read about accepting, choosing, and taking action, what did your mind do? Maybe it said, *How overly simplistic! It's just not possible to accept, choose, and take action.* Maybe right now you're thinking, *Sure, well, I've tried that. It didn't work.* Here's the question to ask yourself now: In a world where it *is* possible to fully cherish and appreciate your child and to have a rich relationship with him—even in his most challenging, frustrating, crazy-making moments, even when you think you cannot stand a particular situation for one more minute—would you want that? Think about that possibility for a moment.

Remember, there are things that you can control, and there are things that you can't. Your mind will continue to be your worst critic—sometimes quietly and sometimes so loudly that you think you can't stand it anymore. However, as we've suggested, you can't control what your mind tells you. Your mind is what it is. It's tempting to engage in a struggle with your mind, and, as you've seen, there are costs to engaging in that struggle. You can, however, make choices in how you behave with and toward your child.

What this book will *not* teach you is how to feel better about yourself as a parent. We as humans all have minds that taunt us, that tell us we aren't enough, and that tell us if people ever found out how incompetent we really were, they'd head for the hills. This is part of the glue that binds us together. It's a great leveler: we all have minds that work this way, whether we're clinical psychologists, parenting experts, struggling parents, or all three. Once we get that notion on the table, we can begin honest, effective work toward our most precious, most valued goals for our children and families. What this book will teach you is that, as one of our dearest mentors often says, "There is as much life and richness in a moment of suffering as in a moment of joy." We hope this book will teach you to feel more fully, to accept your feelings more sensitively and compassionately, and to learn skills that will help you parent more effectively.

Summary

In this chapter, we gave an overview of how acceptance and commitment therapy (ACT) can be used with tried-and-true parenting techniques in early childhood, especially with challenging behaviors. We discussed an ACT philosophy of parenting in which your thoughts and feelings are at the heart of how you perceive and respond to your child.

In the coming chapters, we'll show you how to harness your thoughts and feelings—rather than fighting with them—to sensitively and compassionately parent your young child. In the next chapter, you'll learn about parenting challenges common in the early childhood years. These challenges are points at which your mind may be particularly likely to step in and begin its commentary on your child's behavior—and your parenting. By helping you to gain a full awareness of these challenges and your mind's responses, you'll be better able to effectively use the mindfulness skills taught in later chapters in the service of your values.

CHAPTER 2

Parenting a Child in the Early Years Is Tough Work

Common Challenges

Before you go ahead and have children, find a couple who are already parents and berate them about their methods of discipline, lack of patience, appallingly low tolerance levels, and how they have allowed their children to run riot. Suggest ways in which they might improve their child's sleeping habits, toilet training, table manners, and overall behavior. Enjoy it—it will be the last time you have all the answers.

Colin Bowles, "The String Bag & Octopus Guide to Parenting"

Do you ever worry that your child is developmentally on track? Does he know all of his letters? Can she write her name? Will she be smart? Are the behavior problems he's having serious or will they go away? All children develop at different paces, and there is incredible variety in what is considered "normal" development. Yet for some parents, worries about whether their child has reached this or that developmental milestone can be extremely anxiety-provoking and can lead to pushing a child, perhaps beyond the child's capabilities. It's critically important to provide all children with rich environments and stimulating or challenging activities. However, it's a different matter when childhood becomes a competition to see whose child can reach the finish line first.

Child development isn't always a smooth process. You may have expectations about how things will go and how you'll respond to and nurture your child along the way. However, certain key points of development in young children may present particular challenges for you as a parent. In other words, these developmental "hot points" provide opportunities for your growth as a parent. They may also create stumbling blocks that set you off-kilter. How you feel about these hot points—what you think about them and the meanings you attribute to them—strongly influence how you choose to parent. In ACT, the psychological impact your thoughts and feelings have on your parenting choices is also a function of *context*. Simply put, "context" means what's going on at any particular time for you as a parent, for your family, and for your child in her current stage of development.

In this chapter, we'll explore three different aspects of parenting hot points that occur in early childhood. First, we'll discuss developmental milestones and challenging behaviors common in children ages two through eight—and we'll look at how parents and children commonly experience this period. Second, we'll discuss what happens if you're concerned that your child's behaviors during these hot points signal a significant problem for you. We'll also cover assessment and treatment resources available if you need to seek professional help for your child's behavior problem. Third, to assist you in determining what will be most helpful to you and your child, we'll discuss the advantages and disadvantages of these resources. In light of these issues, we'll highlight the useful tools ACT provides to help you deal with your personal hot points as you nurture your child through these common developmental challenges.

Let's begin with a story describing a typical early childhood situation that goes awry.

❧ Bedtime Story

Alicia, a first grader, is learning to read—and reading has become part of her bedtime routine. Bedtime is a special time for her to spend with her father, Tom. Although she finds reading hard, and she isn't the best in her class, Alicia tries really hard to learn, especially with her bedtime stories. Last night Alicia struggled to read as her father held the book open for her. "T...t-together, the...bears...wan... wand... w...wander..." "Wandered," Tom said quickly, hating how terse his own voice sounded. "Wandered," Alicia said, her body tensing a bit, "d...down the... for...for..." "Forest," Tom said quickly. "Why don't I just read it for you?" he said. Alicia grew still. After a pause, she quietly folded up the book. "It's okay, Daddy. I can try more tomorrow." Tom saw how she crumpled as she leaned away from him. "I'm an idiot," he thought. "I just ruined that for her."

Guiding Your Child Through Developmental Challenges

All parents have moments when they feel that they've not acted in the way that might be most beneficial for their child. Undoubtedly you've had these moments too. These times may be especially frequent as you navigate the early childhood years. The early childhood years are a time of many changes and rapid growth and are a test for all parents—not just you. Just as your child masters the skills for one step of development, she enters a new phase. During the preschool years, your child starts doing new things and demanding more independence and autonomy. She learns words like "no!" and "why?" and uses them with abandon. As she passes into the primary school years, she grows more sophisticated in how she seeks and develops friendships with other children and acquires new academic skills. On the brink of this new phase, some children hesitate and cling to their parents. Others launch off into their new social worlds easily—so independently that you may feel utterly abandoned and wish they were little again.

On top of all this, your child may experience some common behavioral challenges that typically develop in early childhood. These can include tantrums, aggression, defiance, problems with learning to make and keep friends, and disruptive behavior. Or perhaps your child struggles with separation or bedtime fears, or he needs excessive reassurance. Here's the rub: most young children typically experience these behavioral issues occasionally, at one point or another. These struggles tend to come and go. You can handle these moments in ways that are helpful or in ways that inadvertently make them worse. Of course, your mind probably has a lot to say about what your child is going through, as well as how, and how well, you handle that. You—as all parents do—may worry about what such behaviors mean for your child, or whether your parenting helps your child or just makes things worse.

Take a moment now to try the following exercise. It will help you call to mind some of your own parenting hot points: times when you may have struggled with how to handle a developmental challenge presented by your child's behavior. Write your responses in your parenting journal.

EXERCISE: When You Have Reached Your Limit

At least once in a while, all parents have difficult interactions with their children, times when they feel they've reached their limit. Think of one or two experiences with your child that have challenged you as a parent or made you feel as though you weren't sure what to do or what parenting strategy to try. For example, perhaps you told your son to do something and he refused, or you attempted to put your daughter to bed, and she continued to whine and delay. Write them down now, in as much detail as you can. We will come back to the situation(s) you describe later in this chapter.

With the constant changes in early childhood, it's impossible for you as a parent to remain unchanged in how you nurture and guide your child. In short, parenting changes you. If all goes well, you also change your parenting in response to your child's development. Each developmental transition offers opportunities for growth or potential for conflict for both you and your child. For example, when your child was a toddler, you might have "toddler-proofed" your home so that he couldn't get into things that could harm him or reach fragile items he could break. You might have also used distraction to redirect him from seeking out developmentally inappropriate play objects. However, if your child is now a preschooler, he's more curious, mobile, and persistent. He has likely learned to resist redirection, and your distraction ruse may no longer work. So now what do you do? Moments like these challenge you to both learn new ways to parent and let go of parenting strategies that are comfortable and familiar but may no longer be effective. This can be a joyful process, full of wonder and awe. But it can also be difficult and stressful because you go from feeling like you know what you are doing to feeling like a beginner all over again.

It's important to give yourself room to learn and to make mistakes. Learning how to respond to your child's developmental transitions can be a trial-and-error process. Just as your child's development may occur in fits and starts, so may your development of new parenting skills. At times, you'll get stuck acting in ways that are unhelpful to you and to your child. And even when you're aware that you're stuck, you may not know how to get unstuck. Sometimes you may even feel that it's impossible to get things right.

During times like these, it's natural to feel vulnerable and unsure of yourself. Parenting stress during this phase of childhood is common, and given the incredible demands of your young child's development, you may find it hard to cope at times. As your child progresses through predictable developmental stages and demonstrates increasing autonomy, family routines are often disrupted, thereby challenging your confidence in your competence and skills. Though it rarely feels like it at the time, this disruption is often a sign of healthy growth for parents and children alike. These hot points are signs that your child is growing up and that you, as a parent, are noticing and trying to figure out how best to help her do that.

Based on the ACT model, we believe that if you approach parenting hot points in an accepting way, you'll find that it's easier to appreciate, learn, and grow from these opportunities. However, if you react to experiences like this with trepidation or resistance, you're less likely to handle them well. This may set the stage for things to get worse. Your parenting strategies may become more about how to avoid conflict or your child's negative emotion and less about helping your child grow and develop to her fullest potential. You may then begin to see more behavior problems in your child and experience strain in your relationship with her. Simply put, you and your child may experience less joy in one another. To keep that from happening, we'll show you how to turn these challenges into opportunities to connect with your child. Let's begin now by looking at common behavioral challenges that occur at different points in early childhood.

Developmental Hot Points: Age 2 Through 4

An enormous amount of change occurs in children age two through four years. During this period, your child begins to develop his autonomy and to express himself. He also begins to learn about the consequences of his actions. This is a very rewarding age, but it can also be highly frustrating. Let's take a closer look at some common developmental hot points during these years.

Talking, Thinking, and Having Strong Opinions

Around the age of two, your child's language develops rapidly. At this time, she begins to think about—and want—things, even when those things are impossible or unattainable. In short, emerging language and thinking abilities result in your toddler's wanting to do things all by herself. Her enthusiasm for autonomy is often at odds with her limited ability to actually do or get those things. This often leads to the frustrating, tantrum-filled time period referred to as "the terrible twos." This stage is actually a sign that your child is developing well, and it's a signal of her emerging independence.

During this time, children acquire the ability to express themselves at different speeds. Some will speak in few-word sentences or even in single words. Others will have lots and lots to say. How well children are able to express themselves, and how much they feel *understood* by parents, is one major factor in how they behave. For example, when your child wants a specific toy, or to play a game or have a snack prepared in a particular way, and cannot explain this, it's incredibly frustrating. You, too, often feel at a loss because sometimes it's hard to understand why, after you've explored every possible nuance of your child's request, that your little tyrant is still upset. As Ralph Waldo Emerson said, "Children are all foreigners." For you, it's almost like traveling to a foreign country where you don't understand the language. And the stakes are often high: we're socialized to understand that good parents comprehend and are responsive to their children's needs. So what about when that doesn't work the way it's supposed to? How can you be sensitive and nurturing if you can't figure out what your child needs? Consider the following story.

❧ *Getting Ready in the Morning*

Sarah is getting Sam, her three-year-old, ready for the day. She's running a little late for work, and Sam is groggy and slow to rise. He whines and resists getting out of bed, and Sarah watches the minutes tick away as she attempts to coax him into his clothes for preschool. As the minutes tick by, her body becomes more and more tense; her chest tightens.

"No, Mommy, not that shirt!" He sticks his lower lip out and crosses his arms across his chest. "How about this one?" "No!" "This one?" "NO!" Sarah is getting frustrated now and is trying very hard to keep her cool. The many things she has to do before she leaves home and upon arrival at work race through her mind. What will her employer think if she's late again? She starts pulling shirts from Sam's drawer haphazardly and showing them to Sam one after another. "This one?" "NO!" Sam collapses in tears. Sarah still has to feed him breakfast, pack a lunch, and do a dozen other things. "Listen, Mister! You are PUTTING THIS SHIRT ON whether you like it OR NOT!" "I WON'T!" Sam lunges at her, hands balled into fists, and then runs from the room, sobbing. Sarah feels as though an electric shock has passed through her. Now Sam will be impossible to calm. She'll be really late. She's been warned before—what will her employer say? Her chest hurts; she is so anxious and angry with Sam. And she's angry with herself. A thought races through her mind: a good mother would've handled this better.

Sam clearly had something in mind that he wanted, but he couldn't communicate it to his mother. As a result, Sarah tried different options, and she grew frustrated as none of them worked. Her frustration, in turn, may have short-circuited her ability to think through better options to manage Sam's behavior. The interaction escalated into something much more serious and upsetting for both Sam and his mother. In this situation, Sarah could have done things a bit differently. In particular, she could have set an empathic yet firm limit on Sam's refusals. She might have tried presenting two possible shirts and asking Sam to choose one. Limiting the number of choices would be more appropriate to Sam's level of development—too many choices can be overwhelming for a tired, cranky child of his age. If Sam refused to make a choice, she could have said calmly, "I'm going to count to three. If you do not choose one, I will choose for you," and then she would follow through with her proposed course of action.

Limit Setting

Between the ages of two and four, children discover, with great joy, the word "no." Suddenly they realize that they have the ability to choose whether to comply with a request like "Let's clean up your toys" or not. What a concept! This is an amazing freedom! Many children thoroughly enjoy asserting their newly developed independence. They come into their own: they emerge from utter dependence on their parents and become little beings trying to be the masters of their own fate. Then comes stubbornness, resistance to limit setting, and argumentativeness. For parents, this can be a very frustrating time. It's also a critical time when children begin to understand that there are consequences for their behaviors. As a parent, you play a central role in the development of that understanding through your actions. For example, if you give a direction to your child, it's important to make sure that he follows through and that he understands that it's not okay to ignore or resist you. In later chapters, we will teach you how to give consequences for both good and bad behavior. For now, however, it's important to simply understand that your following through is crucial during situations like toilet training, eating, sleeping, and going to school.

Potty Time

Toilet training typically occurs during the years from ages two through four. You have many decisions to make, such as when to begin toilet training and how to fit it into your busy schedule. If you must rely on child care outside the home, this issue of timing is complicated, as some day-care centers may not take children who are not toilet trained. Thus there's often some outside pressure to accomplish this goal. Anecdotal advice abounds: *Boys are harder to potty train than girls. Children should be trained when they are younger than two. Parents should not use pull-up diapers. Parents should use pull-ups, but only at night. Potty training can occur in a day. Potty training takes weeks.* It can be confusing to carefully evaluate all the conflicting advice that you're offered. It may also be hard for you to stick to your own methods in the face of well-meaning friends who may have already toilet trained their children or are trying to unsuccessfully.

Eating and Mealtime Behavior

Children ages two through four are often picky eaters. Having graduated from toddlerhood into the wilds of preschool, they're also learning more independent, appropriate mealtime behavior—or not. Many parents tell us they must chase their children down to feed them. With others, they must give repeated directions *not* to eat spaghetti with fingers AND by all means *not* to wipe it up and down one's shirt. Numerous other parents have expressed the concern that their children are not getting enough nutrition or calories. Some kids are on the "beige diet"—that is, pasta, cereal, and white toast. Other kids are little adventurers who will eat brie, kalamata olives, and hummus under the smug watch of their parents. Whatever the case for you and your child, this can be a tough time—especially in restaurants when your child is the runner, spiller, or spaghetti-sauce wiper. During this phase, it's important for children to get adequate nutrition, and it can be very worrisome for you when you have battles with your child over mealtimes. Some research has even shown that family mealtime behaviors are indicative, in part, of how well a family functions together, as a system (Dickstein et al. 1998; Fiese 2006; Larson, Wiley, and Branscomb 2006). And yet at this age, when parent influence is so critical, mealtimes may be extraordinarily difficult.

Sleeping

Just as adequate nutrition is critical to children's cognitive development, sleep is equally important. Yet bedtime is another common issue around which conflict can arise. Many children in this age group resist bedtime, as they are quickly becoming more autonomous. Sometimes the issue is difficulty separating from their parents at bedtime, which can lead to an extended bedtime ritual that ultimately leaves both parties feeling exhausted. For other families, the issue centers on middle-of-the-night visitation, when children resist staying in their own bed, and, again and again, end up curled up in their parents' bed. For families who practice family bed, which is less typical in the United States than in other countries and cultures, parents may have to cope with the consternation of other parents who believe that teaching children to be more self-reliant is of utmost importance. Yet research suggests that one thing is increasingly clear: especially at this age, children need good *sleep hygiene*, which means consistent bedtime routines and adequate sleep quality and duration (Goodlin-Jones and Anders 2004). If children don't get adequate sleep, they won't function as well during the day. Problem behaviors common in early childhood—such as tantrums, stubbornness, and whining—

can be exacerbated when children are not well-rested. Of course, parents don't function very well when tired either.

Going to School

As children transition into day-care and preschool settings, some resist separating from their parents. Leaving a sobbing, tear-stained child in day care despite repeated entreaties like "Please, can I come with you?" or expressed worries such as "But Mommy, I hate it here!" or "I'm scared!" is a huge task for any parent. You may feel that you're abandoning your child, even if teachers reassure you that the crying only lasts a few minutes. To *not* stay to help your child engage in the classroom activities does not feel like the right thing to do. Thus, you linger, and sure enough, the crying continues or worsens. This can be a difficult situation to negotiate, and it constitutes a very common hot point for children and parents.

Developmental Hot Points: Age 5 Through 8

If children two through four years learn to say "no," kids five through eight have become proficient users of the word "but." Rather than simply refusing to do what they're told, children at this age will give you the reasons why they won't do it. The newly acquired phrases "But I just ..." or "But I didn't ..." provoke many arguments or yelling matches between parents and their children. If, over time, you give demands in harsh, angry ways and your child responds, you may get the message that you should continue issuing demands in this negative way. Or perhaps rather than yelling, you give in to your child's refusal. Either way, this can lead to children's continued resistance to following directions.

In short, your child's emerging pattern of using more sophisticated reasoning and language skills may hook you. Getting hooked is rarely helpful, as the pattern of yelling—where neither one of you listens to the other—simply escalates. When this happens, you may find it hard to put on the brakes and wait for a "teachable moment" to come along when you can speak openly to your child in a way that she feels heard and understood.

Entering School

At this age, children begin to transition to kindergarten and first grade. One issue that commonly re-emerges at this time is separation difficulties. Even when children have adjusted well to a preschool or day-care setting, these separation issues may crop back up. You may worry that your child is "regressing." Resistance to going to school or to separating from parents may manifest in different ways in different children. Some may suffer silently, while others may sulk and mope. As is true for children at any point, their capacity for coping with difficulty is variable. Sometimes they are more resilient, sometimes less so.

You may worry what resistance to going to school means for your child: *Will he be okay? Will she learn to hate school? What if the other kids make fun of him? What if teachers are unsupportive of her?* Worries such as these may lead you to engage in a variety of strategies to "help" your child. These can include your "lingering" in the classroom, or perhaps you might try to minimize or ignore teasing that your child may experience. Sometimes you might avoid the situation entirely, especially if you're uncomfortable speaking with teachers or principals. Unfortunately such tactics often backfire. However, it can be hard to figure out what to do with all of your worries and expectations as you help your child transition to the classroom setting.

Learning to Read

One key developmental task that begins at this age is learning to read and, more generally, engaging in academic skills more independently. There's a wide range of variability in how children learn—in their motivation, pace of learning, and level of interest. Some children persist despite frustration, while others give up. Some breeze through with no trouble at all. For parents concerned about their children's academic success, this can be a very stressful time. Given that learning experiences during the early childhood years are foundational and set the stage for future achievement, you may take many different measures to help your child do well. Some of these might be helpful, and some might not. What works for one child may not work for another, and even though other parents or teachers may have lots of advice for how to help, it may be hard to discern what motivates individual children.

Common Behavior Problems: When Should You Seek Help?

Although the developmental hot points and transitions we describe above occur in nearly all children, some behavior problems emerge in early childhood that are especially concerning and may merit professional help in certain situations. Here we'll talk about two groups of problematic behaviors: acting out ("externalizing behaviors") and difficulties coping with sadness, worries, and fears ("internalizing behaviors"). Research shows that parental response to early externalizing behaviors is key in long-term outcomes; parents who learn to positively interact with their children while consistently applying rules, structure, and consequences tend to have children whose behaviors improve. Some data show that such positive parenting is difficult for parents to carry out if they have a lot of stressful things in their lives or if they're emotionally distressed (Kazdin and Whitley 2006).

Acting-Out Behaviors

Acting-out behaviors, or *externalizing behavior problems*, refer to a set of behaviors that include aggression toward caregivers or peers, difficulty following directions (also called "noncompliance"), argumentativeness, and impulsivity. While the vast majority of children may show some of these behaviors now and then, they tend to come and go. However, if your child acts this way frequently, over time, this can be a problem. Serious acting-out behaviors, if left untreated, have been shown to lead to many poor outcomes in school and in family and peer relationships. We'll describe acting-out behaviors in more detail below.

Aggressive behavior can include hitting, kicking, spitting, biting, pushing, or grabbing toys from peers. It can also include verbal aggression, such as cursing, name-calling, or screaming at peers or parents. Children may become aggressive when fighting over toys, when they feel slighted, or when resisting doing what they are told. Some children, as they get older, tend to bully others to get what they want. Many things contribute to aggression, including watching other children or adults behave this way, feeling victimized by others, or lacking skills in how to problem-solve or negotiate conflicts. Sometimes, unfortunately, aggression helps children get what they want. If that's the case, children tend to continue their aggressive behavior.

Noncompliance, or the failure to follow directions, tends to happen in situations in which parents or caregivers place a lot of demands and/or when demands are placed with poor timing. For example, if you ask your child to clean his room when he's in a bad mood, he might be too upset to comply. Sometimes children don't do what they're told because parents make demands in developmentally insensitive ways. For example, in our interactions with other adults, we may string many directions together: think about the simple act of ordering a coffee at an upscale coffee shop. When giving directions to children, parents might give multiple-step directions without attention to children's developmental capacity for memory and reasoning. Moreover, for whatever reason, sometimes parents forget to praise children when they follow directions. Behavior that goes unpraised tends to decrease over time.

Argumentativeness and noncompliance tend to go hand in hand as children enter kindergarten and the early school years. Your child may argue when you set limits. For some children, this behavior becomes so pronounced that interactions with parents become very negative. As a parent, you may respond to this by relaxing limits, which in turn fuels a child's tendency for argument and whining.

Impulsivity refers to acting without thinking. When impulsivity becomes severe, it can manifest in different ways, such as a tendency toward injuries, interrupting others, or disrupting class. Impulsive children also don't tend to follow directions well, nor do they attend to social cues in interactions with other kids their age. They also may struggle with deficits in *executive functioning*, which means that they have difficulty attending to, processing, and enacting responses appropriate to the information or directions that they are given. Thus, by its very nature, impulsivity is associated with inattention and argumentativeness as well.

The vast majority of children who show these behaviors transition out of them with a little help from their parents. For some children, though, it's not easy to get out of these patterns. For children who display these behaviors more severely and are impaired by them, these problems may persist, and even worsen, over time. When this happens, the child often shows a decreased ability to handle frustration, and she displays moodiness and irritability. If these behaviors begin to interfere with family, friendships, or school, or cause significant distress, it's very important to seek help. Early treatment can be very effective for most families. To determine if you and your child need professional help to deal with externalizing behavior, answer these questions:

- When did your child's externalizing behavior start?

- Has her behavior gotten any better or worse over time?

- Does his behavior harm or affect his relationships with siblings or peers in day care or during playdates? Does it interfere with learning?

- Do you feel so overwhelmed when you think about her externalizing behavior that you cannot come up with or follow through with positive parenting behaviors?

Severe behavior—that which impairs social relationships, learning, and getting along with family—is of great concern. Young children who are frequently or severely aggressive tend to persist in displaying acting-out behaviors and have emotional problems as they get older (Loeber et al. 2000). This is especially true if the child has social-skill problems and cannot make or keep at least one good friend. When such problems persist, become pervasive, and cause significant disruption and distress, they can potentially bring about continued and escalating difficulties. Externalizing behaviors of this severity are beyond the scope of this book. If you're concerned about your child, we encourage you to seek professional help. (See The Process of Getting Professional Help below.)

Worries and Fears

Internalizing behavior problems, or behaviors that are less apparent, are emotional problems that children struggle with "on the inside," possibly without anyone even knowing. Internalizing behaviors include mood issues, such as depression, as well as worries and fears, or anxiety. In this book, we'll focus primarily on the latter, although we'll touch briefly upon depression in young children. It wasn't until very recently that these issues were recognized as occurring at problematic, or "clinically significant," levels in young children. This lack of recognition is due in part to the lack of research in young children and in part because it may be difficult to detect these issues as, by their nature, they may not be obvious to an outside observer.

Depression refers to a set of issues including sad mood, irritability, difficulty concentrating, social withdrawal, failure to find pleasure in things, feelings of hopelessness and worthlessness, and sometimes thoughts of self-harm. There's very little research on depression in young children, although lately many more scientists are paying close attention to this. A series of recent studies by Joan Luby and colleagues (2003; 2004; 2006) have found that preschoolers who met clinical criteria for depression tended to have symptoms that were fairly stable over time and to have family members who also experienced depression. They also exhibited social impairment and reported negative mood and emotions. Sometimes young children struggling with depression also reported physical problems, although these aren't as frequent and certainly are not sufficient to give a diagnosis.

Whether your child experiences depression can be hard to assess. Is your child depressed, or, as is common in children, does his mood just shift a lot? In a similar vein, children in this age group often have trouble describing how they're feeling, which makes it hard to tell if they're experiencing significant mood disturbance. If your child experiences a persistent negative mood over a period of weeks or months, especially if this occurs with irritability, social difficulties, and limited interest in activities like play or school, you may want to consider seeking professional advice from a clinical child psychologist with expertise in this area.

Anxiety refers to feelings of fearfulness, accompanied by worried thoughts and physiological symptoms like muscular tension or an upset stomach. Feeling anxious is normal, and it becomes problematic only when it's very intense and interferes with daily functioning. Children who have fears or worries tend to engage in *behavioral avoidance,* which simply means that they avoid situations that are uncomfortable or frightening to them. Over time and across situations, this can severely limit children's ability to participate in meaningful activities; it can also lead to academic difficulties and poor quality of life.

Recently there has been a great deal of research on anxiety in young children. With regard to symptoms of anxiety, it's important to understand the distinction between differences in children's temperament (or their individual characteristics) and levels of anxiety that warrant clinical intervention. Some children are naturally more shy and inhibited, and it's important for parents to remember that this is a normal individual difference. Some children, for example, will be more reluctant than others when it comes to seeking out new experiences. Some children are very slow to warm up to peers and teachers. That's okay.

Some work suggests, though, that when children have worries and fears that affect their ability to engage socially in the classroom, they may be at risk for developing more prolonged anxiety issues as they grow. Therefore, if you're concerned that your child is overly shy, you should certainly seek professional advice. So to determine whether you should seek professional help for your child's worries and fears, consider the following:

- When did your child's worries or fears start?

- Has her behavior gotten any better or worse over time?

- Do his worries and fears cause him to avoid situations or people that are important to him, such as friends in day care or school? Does his anxiety interfere with learning, or with making and keeping friends at school?

- Do you feel so overwhelmed when you think about her worries and fears that you cannot come up with or follow through with positive parenting behaviors?

As is the case with externalizing behavioral difficulties, many children in this age group express sadness, worry, or withdraw socially at least occasionally. However, these behaviors may be of concern if they cause significant distress to or your child or if they interfere with daily functioning.

The Process of Getting Professional Help

If you're concerned that your child's behaviors warrant professional help, the first step is for you and your child to go for an assessment. An assessment will tell you specifically what's going on for you and your child, as well as give you options for improvement. Often the best place to start is your pediatrician, who will be able to rule out the presence of any physical problems that may explain the symptoms your child is experiencing. After these issues are ruled out, the pediatrician will be able to refer you to appropriate clinical psychologists or mental health providers in your area who specialize in early childhood behavior problems. Your child's school or day care is another place to seek advice on where to find appropriate services.

Once a referral is made, you will likely be asked to come in for a comprehensive assessment. Usually this entails interviews, behavioral checklists completed by you—and, if possible, teachers—and sometimes clinic-based formal tests or behavioral observations in your child's classroom. It's very important to seek a comprehensive assessment, which will tell you—more accurately than a quick screen that consists only of interviews—about how your child is functioning. Many providers, however, use only interviews, which can result in inaccurate diagnoses.

One obstacle that stumps many parents is that it's very difficult to find practitioners who are trained in early childhood emotional and behavioral issues. It's sometimes even harder to find treatment providers who have training in "evidence-based," or researched, treatments for young children. Because of this, some parents may call friends who've "been there and done that" with their own children. Many parents resort to books, magazines, or the Internet for parenting wisdom. While those sources might provide comforting, quick, and easy solutions, the advice you receive may often not be based in fact or be consistent with clinically tested and empirically supported treatments. Carefully evaluate what materials you find and the advice you're given. Of course, throughout this book, we'll provide parenting guidance as well. While this book may be used as a resource if you're struggling with everyday behavior problems, it may also be useful as an additional tool if you're progressing through treatment with your child.

Types of Treatment Available

If a careful evaluation of your child's behavioral difficulties shows that your child needs professional treatment, learn as much as you can about the available treatment options.

Treatments for Acting-Out Behaviors

If your young child struggles with externalizing behavior problems, the gold standard treatment includes *parent behavior management training*, which is based on a substantial body of research. Although many parents may approach treatment with the idea that children go to treatment, therapists work with them, and things turn around, this approach relies on training you, the parent, as a therapeutic coach. Treatment centers very much on helping the family change patterns that may be unhelpful to the child. Children struggling with stubbornness or aggression resist following directions, and they have learned to behave in unpleasant ways to prevent or stop parents from placing demands on them. For example, children with these difficulties often whine or throw tantrums when asked to follow a direction or when limits are placed on their behavior. Research suggests that children experiencing these difficulties tend to become unpleasant for parents to be around, and thus parents may tend to withdraw demands or simply avoid giving directions in order to avoid conflict.

Thus, in parent behavior management training, you learn how to build a positive relationship with your child, how to encourage appropriate behavior, and how to discourage unwanted behavior. Typically this occurs over the course of several weeks to months. It's important to understand that the techniques taught in treatment are not things that can be attempted and then abandoned when change occurs. They are skills that must be learned and flexibly used over the course of your child's development. When treatment doesn't work, it's often because the skills are ineffectively learned, inconsistently used, or abandoned over time.

Treatments for Worries and Fears

Research suggests that behavioral and cognitive-behavioral treatments are useful with children who experience separation issues or anxiety. In a manner similar to treatments for externalizing behaviors, parents of young children are often taught to be therapeutic coaches to help encourage their children to face their fears. For example, recent work suggests that parents are helpful in supporting their children in developing "bravery-based" behaviors, as in the treatment developed by Donna Pincus and colleagues at Boston

University (2005). Parents are coached in how to support their children's skill in developing more effective ways of coping with their anxiety when separated from their parents at school or camp. Comparable approaches are helpful in working with children with other anxiety-based behaviors. The core ingredient of these treatments is what is called *exposure,* which, simply put, means facing your fears. This entails the collaborative development of a hierarchy of situations in which the child becomes fearful. Once the therapist, parent, and child have created a hierarchy, the family members are taught skills for how to cope with the child's fears and to encourage the child to willingly approach, rather than avoid, his fears. However, as with parent behavior management training, remember that the skills learned are not supposed to be temporary. Rather they're meant to be used throughout a child's development to support continued growth and to support improvements made in treatment.

Is It My Fault?

Sometimes parents who seek treatment for their children and who are taught skills to help their children feel they're at fault for their children's psychological difficulties. Remember, though, that children bring to the table their own personalities, capacities for learning, and resistance or willingness to change. Thus, it's never your fault for "making" your child turn out the way she does. However, you do have opportunities to make an enormous difference in helping or hindering your child in learning different ways of being. Early childhood is perhaps the most critical of those times—the time when you might stand to have the most impact. It isn't helpful to think in terms of "fault"; it is helpful to think in terms of possibility: you may choose the role of helping your child have rich, meaningful, nurturing experiences on the long and meandering way to growing up.

When you come up against your child's behavior problems, you confront many expectations: your own, your child's, and those of friends, family, and other parents. Most of the treatments discussed above deal with these expectations in a limited way, if at all. In short, although the treatments can be very effective, they don't explicitly deal with the experience of parenting. This may explain, at least in part, why such treatments tend to work best for families without significant stressors beyond their children's behavioral issues. For example, these treatments don't tend to work well for parents who have other demands on their time, who may be struggling with depression or worry themselves, or who suffer financial hardships or substance-use issues. Ironically, parents struggling with these issues are the ones who most need help and support.

Why ACT Is a Good Treatment Model

As we mentioned earlier, what parents think and feel may be of critical importance in how effectively parents nurture and guide their children. Parents of young children who cope with multiple stressors, such as financial hardship and symptoms of anxiety, depression, and stress, are likely to engage in experiential avoidance as a coping strategy (Shea, Sims, and Coyne 2007; Silvia and Coyne 2009; Coyne and Thompson 2009). Experiential avoidance, which we touched on in the first chapter, refers to a tendency to avoid, manage, ignore, or otherwise control unwanted or painful thoughts, feelings, and bodily sensations. In fact, parents who rely more on experiential avoidance as a coping strategy are more likely to perceive parenting as stressful and to report using more punitive and inconsistent parenting strategies (Shea, Sims, and Coyne 2007). Although our research is preliminary, it highlights the importance of attending to your *experience* of parenting as well as your *skills* in parenting.

As a treatment "model," ACT helps you notice your thoughts and feelings without overreacting to them. It is a *behavioral* approach, which means it highlights your actions and their consequences, especially those that will help you move toward what you really care about for you and your child. Since ACT is meant to help you notice your thoughts and feelings and help you pursue your values, it can guide you as you deal with typical behavioral challenges in your young child and, in conjunction with other behavioral treatments, also assist you with more severe problems. To begin to notice your thoughts and feelings in parenting situations, try the following exercise.

EXERCISE: Noticing Your Feelings

Think of a difficult interaction with your child; it can be the same one you wrote about in the previous exercise or a different one. See if you can open your mind to those remembered experiences, and walk back through them as an observer, as if you're watching a movie of it happening.

■ What are you thinking?

■ What are you feeling?

■ How does your body feel?

Write down your thoughts in your parenting journal.

Was it difficult to remember what you felt in the "movie" you imagined? Or did the thoughts and feelings arise easily? What was it like noticing those feelings again in retrospect rather than when you were actually in that moment with your child?

In the following chapters, you'll learn how to gain some distance from the thoughts and feelings you have in situations like the one above. In ACT, gaining some distance from your thoughts and feelings—so they don't control your actions—is called *defusion*. Throughout this book, we'll help you practice defusion (and other ACT techniques) so you can move forward in your life, in the direction of what you care about most for you and your child.

Summary

This chapter focused on common challenges and hot-button developmental issues that provide opportunities for you to grow—or stumble—as you build a repertoire of sensitive, responsive parenting skills. We addressed issues in children age two through four years as well as those five through eight. One major goal of this chapter was to help you see that all families go through parenting hot points, especially in early childhood. Finally, we discussed externalizing and internalizing behaviors, highlighting that many children experience fleeting issues with these. When such behaviors, however, cause significant distress or impairment, it's time to seek professional help. ACT can be used as a standalone treatment for children experiencing normal behavior problems, or it can augment other approaches. Specifically it can help you defuse from difficult thoughts and emotions that may get in the way of effective parenting.

CHAPTER 3

Parenting Values

What Matters Most

Wheresoever you go, go with all your heart.

Confucius

Parenting can feel quite overwhelming and stressful, especially when there's a struggle involved. You may have become, especially in difficult moments, what we call "the knee-jerk parent." When your child whines or is defiant, you may simply react without thought or consideration. If your struggles with your child have continued over time, as they do for many parents, parenting may seem like a string of these knee-jerk moments. After such moments, you may feel remorseful, or your mind may scold you with self-insulting thoughts. Your mind might even give you a brief slide show of what a "good" parent might have done or, worse, an instant replay of how you might have been perceived by other parents looking on. And when you try to turn your mind off (and who wouldn't?), you might find the thoughts or images becoming more persistent. Your tension level probably increases. When this happens, life for you as a parent likely feels restrictive and negative, and you may feel worn-out or hopeless. Read the story below as an example.

✤ This Is All Your Fault—Go Away!

Carrie, a stay-at-home mom, has a six-year-old son named Carson and a daughter, Bella, who is almost two. Recently everyone in their family had the flu. All of them felt awful, and the children were cranky. Carrie felt overwhelmed from caring for them, and disciplining them, all day long. She was ill herself and became exhausted.

She put a pot of soup on the stove, hoping that eating would help everyone feel better, and then she accidentally fell asleep on the couch.

Carson, who'd helped his mother in the kitchen before, recognized the sound of the soup boiling over. He tried to wake his mother but couldn't, so he went to turn off the soup by himself. He pulled a chair over toward the stove so that he could reach the knob, and he successfully turned it off. However, he didn't notice that Bella had toddled in behind him. She tried to climb up to the stove and turn the knob just like her big brother. When she reached forward, she lost her balance. She didn't really get hurt, but she did tumble to the floor, screaming.

Bella's screams woke her mother, who began interrogating Carson about what had happened. Carson said, "I couldn't wake you up, and I heard that the soup needed to be turned off, and …" Carrie cut him off. Her face was red, she grabbed him, and she yelled at him, "Your sister got hurt. This is all your fault—just go away, get out of here, NOW!"

Carson began to cry and almost immediately Carrie's guilt set in. She started thinking things like "He was just trying to help," "At least no one got burned—really Bella was just more scared than anything," "I am so horrible; I yelled at him for doing the right thing." "If I hadn't fallen asleep, none of this would have happened." Then her mind got louder: "You're an awful parent. Don't you know that you can't sleep and leave the kids unattended, ever—that's just not okay, stupid!" Carrie was both mad at herself and worried about her children's feelings. She wanted to talk to them, but she felt that she didn't know how. So she went back to the couch and turned on the TV.

Moments like this happen to all parents. When something like this happens to you, you may have a hard time answering the question "Why did I ever become a parent?" This is especially likely if your child's behavioral issues have been building over time or if you're particularly worried about them, for whatever reason. You can get so caught up in the moment that it's difficult to step back and see what direction you're going—as a parent, as a member of a family, or as an individual. In other words, it may feel as if you have lost your compass, which gives you a sense of direction and purpose. Your moment-to-moment interactions with your child may simply be geared toward *stopping* whatever negative situation is going on, which causes you to lose sight of the big picture. Many parents are more interested in meeting an immediate goal in their interaction with their children—for example, stopping a tantrum or whining—than they are in focusing on long-term goals, such as enjoying activities together as a family. Longer-term outcomes can easily get lost in the mayhem of the daily struggle and begin to feel beyond reach. When this is the case, just being around your child can lead to tension or a sense of pressure. At the darkest moments, parenting may not occur to you as a choice that you have made but rather as something you have fallen into, something that you must do—no matter how tired, uninspired, or unsure you might be feeling. It may be all you can do to just make it through the day.

Focusing on what's most important to you—about your child, about being a parent, and about caring for your family and yourself—is what this chapter is about. Determining and remembering these things, we hope, will serve as a compass, giving you a sense of direction and purpose in your parenting, even in your most difficult moments. In ACT, those things that we care most about are called *values*.

When Life Gets in the Way of Focusing on Values

As a parent of a young child, you probably find it hard to remember the last time you sat back and considered the things that are truly important to you. If you're like most parents, your values have likely gotten lost in the tasks of daily living—routines of waking your child, getting meals for him, helping with homework, or putting her to bed. Who has time to think about bigger-picture things? Taking time to do that may seem like a distant luxury.

And again if you're like most parents, when parenting becomes difficult, you may feel as if you're just going through the motions. How does this manifest on a physical level? You may feel exhausted and overwhelmed or experience a sort of heaviness. Or you may feel numb and checked out, or perhaps you have a sense of urgency and feel trapped. Consider these feelings as you do the following exercise. Write them down in your parenting journal.

EXERCISE: Knee-Jerk Parenting

Remember a time when you've felt stretched too thin. What happened when you struggled to manage your child's misbehavior? What feelings showed up? Did your feelings color the entire interaction?

If you could describe those moments as "spaces," would they feel roomy and expansive or small and cramped, areas in which you must fight to get out?

Quite likely, you experience a sort of tunnel vision when you get into situations like these. Your only goal is to do whatever is necessary to stop your child's problem behavior. Your world may narrow to this one interaction, which, you may feel, is the barometer by which you measure your success or failure as a parent. And in that moment, you probably rely on whatever behavior management strategies you're most used to—typically those that lead to short-term success, such as using bribery to get your child to stop arguing. Think back to Carrie who was exhausted and startled awake by Bella's screams. She was worried about her baby's well-being and then, when she found out that Bella was really okay, she was annoyed. She was angry with her son, and she assumed the accident was his fault. So she screamed "Go away, NOW!" to Carson. In the moment, Carrie did what she needed to do, or thought she needed to do, to take control of the situation. Later she realized that it wasn't Carson's fault and she felt like a failure as a parent. Most parents have felt this sense of failure as well as the feelings (concern, anger) that Carrie had when her daughter screamed. And most of us parents don't like feeling those ways, so we do things to try to make those feelings go away just to feel better for a little while. We do this without necessarily thinking about the longer-term consequences. As another example of this tunnel vision, think of the last time that your child whined and begged for a treat in the checkout line at the grocery store. Think of what you did to get her to stop. Did you buy the treat or yell at her to stop whining just so she would be quiet? Unfortunately, although these strategies may be effective immediately, they may also prevent the possibility of long-term gains or more extensive and lasting child behavior changes. Here's a guided meditation exercise to help you explore what this means.

EXERCISE. The Desert Island Metaphor for Parenting

Imagine that you're stranded on a small, tropical island, sitting on the edge of a wide beach, looking out over the ocean as the waves crash onto the shore. Your island has the basic things that you need to survive, including food, water, and shelter. You're able to make fire for heat on cold evenings. When you were shipwrecked here, things were probably very hard at first. You felt the weight of responsibility to take care of yourself and to gain skills you would need to survive. You had to learn where and how to find food, water, and shelter, and how to notice the changing tides and seasons to ensure that you kept safe in the weather. You might have felt frightened, alone, and unsure of yourself.

Now think back to what it was like when you had your first child and brought him home as an infant. You probably felt frightened, alone, and unsure of yourself. You might have experienced a towering sense of responsibility, coupled with self-doubt about your ability to handle things or parent the "right" way. Even if you did your reading, spoke with friends who had children, and called your own parents frequently for advice, you probably still had to learn many things the hard way—all by yourself.

And so it is on your island. After a good deal of time spent learning to live on your island, things may have gotten a bit easier. You may be used to the way things usually go. In fact, you might have been so busy simply learning to survive, the idea of rescue—of getting help or finding populated land—has gotten lost. Maybe you've even let go the possibility of getting off the island. After all, life might not be great, but at least you're managing. And the potential costs of change might be too high: the ocean is rough and full of dangerous currents. There's no certainty you'll be rescued if you attempt to get off the island. And what's more, how exactly would you get off the island? You might not have any idea.

As a parent, you may have a parallel experience. Over time, you probably grew a little more comfortable with the tasks of parenting and began to trust your own competence some. As your child grew older, you may have fallen into a number of knee-jerk patterns to soothe your child or to stop tantrums or whining. And these might work pretty well in the short run. Especially when you're feeling overwhelmed and stressed as a parent or when you're parenting in knee-jerk ways that might help you get by in the short run, you might have some of the same thoughts you'd have if you were on a deserted island. You might have lost hope or given up on things being different and settled on how things are at the moment between you and your child. If things aren't going so well, you might not know how to change them. Or perhaps things are going okay and you're getting things done, taking care of the business of daily child-rearing tasks. Maybe once in a while, you have thoughts about how things could be different or how things might feel more vital, life-giving, or inspired. At that point, your mind might step in with thoughts like *Yeah, when would I have time for that?* or *My life isn't like that* or *I just don't have the energy.* Take a moment to listen to your mind—does any of this feel familiar?

When you consider the possibility of getting off the island, all sorts of questions might flood your mind: *How do I navigate? What direction should I go? How will I build a craft to get myself there? Will I get through huge surf and violent storms and survive dehydration or starvation?* You might also experience a sense of fear or doubt. Perhaps you start to think *Maybe such a place doesn't exist* or worry that even if it does, you won't find it. You might feel as though you would make mistakes that would lead you off course and then leave you worse off than you were before, somewhere lost at sea. Many things might get in your way of getting off the island.

Parenting your young child may often leave you feeling lost and full of doubt, afraid of making mistakes, especially when difficult behaviors arise or in situations in which you doubt your ability to handle your child's behavior effectively. Your mind may chime in with comments like *But I've done everything I know how* or *I already tried that.* The "space" in which you parent may feel very tight and small, devoid of room to move, or even think, freely.

Despite these thoughts, you may have a vague sense of a different direction in which you would like to go. That direction may not be clear, and it may occur to you as a sense that something else—or more—is possible than these struggles with your child. You may not know how to get there, and you may not trust the sense of possibility. At times like these, your mind likes to shut things down. Minds are trained to calculate risk. They encourage (or coerce) you to stick with what you know and focus on short-term goals rather than long-term goals. And that's okay—it's just your mind doing its job. Unfortunately, if what you are parenting *for* is short-term results like simply managing daily events or child behavior problems, you may feel burdened and limited. But what if this isn't "as good as it gets?" What if your experience of parenting could be different—not in terms of *what* you or your child does but rather in terms of your relationship to your own parenting and your child?

Values as Actions

Here's a different idea: what if you could choose how to respond to your child instead of simply reacting to situations as your mind describes them to you? What if you could choose your direction, even when you're reacting to whatever's happening in the moment? Values are *chosen* directions or ways of being. You might think of your values as your *chosen purpose.* They're not destinations but rather points on a compass that guide you through your life. You may not know exactly how to *live* your values, but they can guide you all the same. You see, values are not goals—things to accomplish or places at which to arrive; values are actions guided by what you most care about. That is why we sometimes use the term "valuing" instead of talking about "having values" with our clients. "Valuing" means pursuing those things that are most important to you with integrity. To help you begin to understand what is meant by valuing, do the exercise below.

> ### EXERCISE: How Do You Want
> ### to Be Remembered?

We all get caught up in our lives and often feel we're carried along by a current independent of our wants and desires. Here's an opportunity to experience how you might choose to live in a different way. It may seem a bit dark, but bear with us for a few moments and its purpose will become clear.

Imagine that you've died, and, for some reason, you are able to attend your own funeral as a spirit. No one can see you or hear you, but you can hear everything that people say. Imagine that someone important to you steps up to the front of the room and delivers your eulogy. If this was happening today, how do you think this person would describe you? What would he or she say your life was about, without exaggerating things or trying to make you sound good? Is this eulogy how you would want to be remembered?

Take a few moments to think about that and write your thoughts and responses to each of these items in your journal. Please try not to screen or change them; simply write your thoughts down as they are.

What showed up in your mind when you completed this part of the exercise? If you're like most people, you might have felt some hesitation or even a hint of regret or embarrassment, or you might have experienced some fleeting thoughts like *I'm not sure there are many nice things to say about me.*

Now take a few moments to consider the following questions. When you write your answers in your journal, assume that you're fully able to choose the life you want. Your mind will tell you that you can't, and you should notice that and then put those thoughts aside for a moment. Right now, write about what, deep in your heart, you care about most deeply.

- If you could choose one thing to make your life be about, what would that one thing be?

- If you could choose to make your life and how you lived it be about the things that were most important to you, how would you want to be remembered?

We're guessing that things like "keeping the house clean" or "making sure my child follows directions" were not the first things on your mind. Notice what did show up for you in this exercise. Was it something larger than that? Maybe something like "I would want to be known as a great parent" showed up for you, or maybe it was a thought like "I care about helping people; I hope that gets said about me when I'm gone." Let your mind gently hold it—not as a promise but as a possibility. What would it be worth to you if you could live a life that led to this description of yourself?

What If Pursuing My Values Is Impossible?

As you worked through the exercise above, you may have noticed your mind chiming in with thoughts like *Yeah, right* or *Sure, that would be nice, but it's impossible*. Again, your mind is simply doing its job. It's easier to convince yourself that you don't want something that you care deeply about than to acknowledge that you desire something with your whole heart. Sometimes, as we mentioned earlier, it's hard for parents to even think about the things that are most important to them. That, too, is likely your mind's subtle influence as it attempts to protect you from your fears of failure or loss.

In a speech in 1899, Theodore Roosevelt said, "Far better it is to dare mighty things, to win glorious triumphs—even though checkered by failure— than to take rank with those poor spirits who neither enjoy much nor suffer much, for they dwell in the gray twilight that knows neither victory or defeat." When you let in the things that you care most about—when you "dare mighty things"—your mind quickly engages you in its debate about whether you can—or can't—get what you want. When this happens, see if you can acknowledge those thoughts, just notice them, and set them aside. Would you rather focus on setting a course toward what you care about or fight with your mind? See what happens if you stand up, take action, and move toward what matters most to you.

Values Aren't Goals

Sometimes people confuse values or valued directions with goals. *Goals* are, in and of themselves, endpoints. The difference between a goal and a value is like the difference between traveling to California and traveling west. If your goal is to reach California and you head toward California, sooner or later you will arrive, and your journey ends. If you head west, you could keep going indefinitely in that direction—there is always "more west." Values are like that: they are directions, defined by what you care most about in your life, that you choose. *Valuing* is choosing to live in ways that are consistent with those things that are most important to you. As such, engaging in a valued activity naturally makes you want to do it more. This behavior can be motivating or self-renewing, since values cannot be "reached," but rather they serve to direct your actions (Coyne, Burke, and Freeman 2008).

Many times when we ask parents what they want to work for, they'll mention material things like a better salary or more job security. Sometimes they mention small, immediate, concrete things like wanting their child to do as she is told or to stop whining. Other times people mention very abstract things—for example, that they want to be happier or less stressed in their lives. These are all great examples of goals. However, values give a broader context to our goals: we strive for goals *in the service of* our values. This means we'll work to reach goals that move us closer to what we care about. Think about being a parent. When your children grow up, you're still a parent—there's no end to that journey, even when children move away or start families of their own. The *way* you parent must necessarily change over time; however, the fact that you *are* a parent does not. Similarly, valuing is an activity that never ends, but it gives meaning and purpose to the parenting tasks you accomplish in daily life. It's something you continue to strive for throughout your life and as your children grow and mature.

EXERCISE: Parenting Values and Goals

You picked up this book for a reason, and you've read it thus far because you have something that you want for your child and for yourself. Take a moment now to consider why you're reading.

1. Take out your journal and write down a few key words about your reason for seeking help with your child.

2. See if you can pick out any values or goals from what you just wrote. For example, you might have written that you need to know how to deal with your child's defiance. That would be a goal, because learning how to deal with specific behavior has an endpoint. Or you might have written that you want a meaningful relationship with your child. Think for a minute about whether that would be a value or a goal. It really does not have an ending, because meaningful relationships require ongoing work, so it is more like a value.

3. Allow yourself to consider what you wrote without judging it. It doesn't matter if you wrote about all negative things or if you only wrote about goals. Just notice what thoughts and feelings got put down on paper.

4. Now, if you can think of one, write down a value about parenting. It certainly can apply to you, but it doesn't have to if you can't think about

that now. For example, "I value making a positive difference in my child's life," or "It's important that my child knows that I love him," or "I want my relationship with my daughter to be extraordinary."

5. Moving toward values often requires us to meet certain goals. Think of one or two goals that would help you move toward the value you named in step 4. For example, "I will tell my son every day that I love him" or "I will learn how to properly implement time-out so that my child can learn appropriate behavior." Write your goals in your journal.

Values Aren't Feelings

Sometimes, pursuing your values is really difficult. Take, for example, the value of promoting a healthy lifestyle for your family. Living and promoting a healthy lifestyle are not endpoints in and of themselves. Living this valued goal with integrity might comprise a string of related goals, such as resisting buying or eating foods high in fat or sugar, monitoring your family's meal-portion sizes, or exercising together daily. However, in certain contexts, following this value might become more challenging—for instance, when you're out at a restaurant with friends or in the snack aisle of the supermarket and your hungry child begs for something to eat. It's really easy to give in to temptation at points such as those. When you choose to "give in," you deviate from your values or valued direction—what you consider most important in your life. Sometimes you may not even notice when you go off the course leading to your values. Other times—and there are probably plenty of these—you know you're off course, but you might not *feel* like getting back on course. In fact, returning to your valued direction might feel pretty terrible, and veering off course may feel like a relief, at least for a short while. For example, serving your child a sugary cereal most mornings, even though it's obviously not moving in the direction of promoting a healthy lifestyle, likely feels better than listening to her cry about her egg whites and tofu bacon. There isn't a right or wrong answer in this situation, but simply being aware of your value and recognizing that you're getting off course—without letting your mind judge you for this—is a step toward acknowledging what really matters to you as a parent. And acknowledging your values is an important step toward acting on them.

The Importance of Vulnerability:
The Cost of Values

As with any other choice you make, there are costs and benefits to pursuing the things that are most important to you. When you as a parent pursue the things that matter most to you, you're probably playing for fairly high stakes. Wanting your child to be healthy and not get sick, for example, probably matters a lot. Failure to attain these ends might be a terrifying proposition for you. If this is the case, as it is for many parents with whom we work, then welcome to being human. To value something is to make yourself vulnerable. The more you really want something or care about it, the harder it would be to lose that thing. In fact, if you're ever curious about whether or not you're pursuing a value, pay attention to how vulnerable or uncomfortable you feel. That's a good sign of how much something matters to you. For example, if you value raising your children in ways that don't perpetuate gender stereotypes— such as "pink is for girls" or "boys don't play with dolls"—then you might feel your blood pressure rising if your daughter comes home in a princess dress and tells you that only boys play baseball.

Many parents report a feeling of vitality, accompanied by sheer terror, as they choose to pursue valued ends. The cost of valuing is, very simply put, to open yourself to hurt, self-doubt, and disappointment in the service of your most treasured pursuits. The only question that matters here is this: in a world where it were possible to choose to be the parent you envisioned in your best moments, would you be willing to risk feeling vulnerable and afraid of losing what matters to you? For example, if you value raising your child in a two-parent family, are you willing to risk the possibility that your relationship may not weather the storm of parenting and at the same time still work toward a healthy, vibrant relationship with your partner?

Remember that valuing—and *not* valuing—is always a *choice*. What you value may change some over time, but remember that valuing has no end—it's a constant process. And, in every moment, it's entirely up to you to choose to seek your values—or not. Just like any other choice that you might make, choosing to pursue your values occurs in the context of how you're feeling at any given moment. And just like any other choice, you can make this one independently of how you're feeling or what you're thinking in that moment. For example, you might feel guilty and even doubt yourself if your child cried about not fitting in with other kids because he has to wear his helmet while bike riding. However, you could still require him to wear the helmet, based on your value of him being safe and healthy. This requires you to step back a bit and consider a bigger, long-term picture. This isn't easy and it won't always feel comfortable, and we'll talk about this more later. For now, know that it's common to feel tugs to behave in opposite directions: "I want him to wear his helmet, but I don't want him to scream and cry and fight me, and I don't want him to be teased by his friends." To live consistently with your values means making choices that steer you toward the things that you feel are most important in your life, regardless of your fears or doubts. Taking a deep breath before you act is a good idea. As a parent, you'll likely have many moments in which you do not feel like parenting. And it's entirely up to you how you handle those moments. Remember, even when parenting feels oppressive and you feel boxed in by the many demands that your young child makes, you have a choice about how you respond as a parent.

Leap and the Net Will Appear

There's a Zen saying: "Leap and the net will appear." That might be a scary idea because you must have great trust that, when you leap or try something different, things will be okay. Again, to live consistently with your values means making choices that steer you toward the things that you feel are most important in your life, regardless of your fears, doubts, or feelings of vulnerability. As a parent, there are many moments in which you'll have to choose "what you want to be about" even when it seems risky. For example, the value of making a positive difference in your child's life might require punishing her for misbehavior, and it may feel like there's a risk of her getting mad and not liking you, and thus you failing to make the difference you want.

Learning how to make such a choice doesn't suggest that you'll always know the right thing to do in a parenting situation. But what this approach does do is help you to choose a purpose in moments that you share with your child. When you string those moments together over time, you may be able to see a clear course. It may not always be straight, and it certainly won't always be easy. Sometimes you may get lost. But once you have identified your chosen values, you have a compass to navigate through the dark waters.

Your Valued Areas of Life: No Right or Wrong

The areas of life that you care about—such as family and career—interact. You have one, whole life, and your behavior in one area affects other areas. So as you consider your values, it's important to pay attention to all areas of your life, including the thoughts and feelings going on inside you and their interplay with what goes on for you at home, at work, and in your personal and family relationships.

Valuing, both within and across life areas, is always done because it serves a purpose—a purpose that is relevant in that moment, in that situation. And values, which are chosen in the moment for a purpose, cannot be evaluated as right or wrong. What we mean by this is that different people care about different things, and sometimes you may care about things to a different degree based on your own situation. For example, you may choose to sleep with your infant because you value being physically close to your child and believe in the developmental benefits of this. Another parent may choose to have her child sleep in his own crib in his own room because she values protecting her intimate relationship with her partner and wants her child to be able to self-soothe at an early age. There's no right or wrong inherent in either of these choices, but values underlie each choice. And, a year from now, each of these parents may make different choices based on changing values and circumstances. There's no judgment to be made about that. What you care about is just as important as what other people care about, and vice versa. No one but you can determine the merits of choosing a value in one life area or situation over another.

At times, you'll feel like your values conflict with one another. And there will be times, in certain situations, when you have to divide your time and attention between various valued life areas (like parenting and career). You'll have to choose how to spend your time and energy. When this happens, consider the bigger picture: the things that you value and work toward tend to balance out over time. For example, while you may have to put your career on a back burner while your children are young, the time will come when your children need you less and you'll be able to refocus on your career, perhaps even putting parenting on a back burner. As Fred Rogers puts it in *The World According to Mr. Rogers*, "You rarely have time for everything you want in this life, so you have to make choices. And hopefully your choices can come from a deep sense of who you are" (2003, 32).

Not surprisingly, you may find your values manifesting themselves in different areas of your life. For example, if you value making a difference for other people, you can act on that in your parenting, your career, and many other areas of life. Some research even indicates that people who can flexibly value several areas of life have better psychological health (Adcock, Murrell, and Woods 2007). Therefore, people who say things like "I can care about my career and my child equally at the same time without feeling angry or guilty" tend to be more emotionally healthy than those who are tied to the idea, for example, that "children always come first to any good parent." Although only you can know what values are important and useful to you, it may be that having multiple areas of life that you care about will give you the sense that you have many more possibilities to do the things that matter to you most.

Learning to Live Your Values

Once you begin to identify your values, how can you tell if you're pursuing them? Your mind will probably continually tell you whether it thinks you're on the right or wrong course. It'll be up to you to decide if your mind is helping you move in a valued direction or whether it's steering you off course. For example, going back to the bicycle-helmet situation, you might think *I am a horrible parent if I make my son wear this thing when none of the other kids are wearing helmets.* You might feel guilty and think you'll just let him go without it. Reacting to those thoughts would mean that you'd let him ride without it to relieve your immediate concerns and uncomfortable feelings. Not reacting to it would mean that you could choose to require him to wear the helmet (or not). Remembering your value of your son being safe and healthy, you'd likely tell him to wear the helmet, even if you feel bad about it. When you notice your mind telling you things about your parenting, try to think about what your parenting values are, and whether your thoughts and feelings are helping you move toward those values or away from them. Making your son wear the helmet would work toward your value of keeping him healthy, for example, whereas the thought that he'll get made fun of only gets in your way. Later in the book, we'll talk more about your mind and what you can do with thoughts that aren't helpful.

At this point, you may find it useful to explore your own values. The following guided meditation exercise, adapted and expanded from work done by J. T. Blackledge (Blackledge and Hayes 2006), focuses on what matters to you. It will help you identify how you might follow your parenting values.

EXERCISE: Moving Toward Your Horizon

Imagine a limitless oceanic skyline. In front of you, the sun rises over the horizon—gold and orange light illuminates the clouds around it. Valuing is like sailing toward the horizon. The horizon is always changing; it may seem to rise or fall, or even seem to move around you at times. Because it's always shifting, you can never reach it—you can only move toward it. When you're heading toward the horizon, you're warmed by the sun's light. You feel vital; the vitamins from the sunlight enrich your body. Perhaps a soothing breeze gently moves along with you. Notice that you do not have to be directly in the path of the rising sun. As long as you head toward the horizon, the sun shines on you and all the things around you. Your behavior doesn't always have to match your values flawlessly; if you are generally heading in the direction of what you want your life to stand for, you will feel the importance in that. It won't always be easy or feel good. Strong winds may blow you around and try to keep you away from your course, and dark clouds will sometimes block your view. Your life circumstances may make it hard to stay on the course, and your mind may tell you that it's not possible. There may be storms: feelings of despair and failure may cover you like rain, and you may lose your way. So it's probably a good idea to lay down some buoys to mark your course. Each buoy, representing a goal or a valued action, shows your progress and can guide you toward your horizon as well.

Goals are important; specific things that you can do to show yourself and those around you what you care about help you stay on your course. Now take a closer look at your own horizon. After each step below, write your thoughts in your parenting journal.

1. What's on your horizon? Remember, the horizon is limitless and there's room for whatever you want to be there—room for your hopes and dreams about parenting and room for whatever you choose for yourself too. Don't focus on the problems that would make it hard to be the way you want to be—just think about yourself in an ideal world, in a world where you could be exactly as you choose to be.

2. Think for a moment about the kind of parent that you want to be. Describe your behaviors with your child and list some of the qualities you would have in your relationship with your child.

3. Now go ahead and let your mind do its work. What thoughts come up regarding your heading to your horizon?

4. What feelings or memories do you notice when you think about moving toward your horizon? Do you feel anything in your body?

5. Now see if you can just notice all of those reactions and put down a buoy. Choose one specific behavior that you're willing and able to do right now, in this moment or in the next interaction with your child, that will move you closer to your values, to your sunrise on the horizon.

6. Think about other buoys that will need to be laid down. Just notice how you feel and what your mind does as you imagine your goals.

Your Mind and Your Heart on the Valued Course

In completing this exercise, you may have noticed your mind chattering away at you. That's why it's important to be able to discriminate between what your mind is telling you and what your heart is telling you. Are your thoughts serving or hindering you? One way to find out is to ask yourself these questions:

■ Does what I'm doing feel *vital*, or does it feel like it's getting in the way of what I care about, draining the life out of it and me?

■ Is my behavior inspiring to me?

Sometimes parents tell us that they know when they're following their values because they experience a sense of lightness where there was a sense of struggle or weight before. As we've already said, it's often unhelpful to think about or evaluate your progress. Rather notice how you feel, how your body feels, and whether this lifts you rather than pressing you down. You might also notice the volume of your mind when you pursue valued ends.

■ Does it get louder or harsher in its warnings or criticisms, or does it quietly cheer you on?

Quite likely when you're working with your child's more challenging behaviors, especially constant defiance, you may sense this heaviness or struggle. Similarly your mind might crank up the volume until it seems impossibly loud. In those moments, slow down, stop what you're doing and notice and appreciate that experience. Consider the following example.

⚘ *Don't Bother Your Sister*

Laura loves being a mom. Being a good parent to her children is very important to her, and she really wants to make sure that she guides her children well, so that they grow up to be mature, loving adults. It's also very important to Laura to enjoy her time with her children when they're young.

One afternoon Laura is in the den working on bills while her two children—Dan, age six, and Caroline, age three—play in the foyer. Dan is building an elaborate castle with his blocks, and Caroline wants to help. Each time she tries to add to Dan's structure, he whines or speaks to Caroline harshly. Laura tries to concentrate on her family's budget but interrupts her work by periodically admonishing Dan: "Dan, I told you not to use that tone with your sister!" "Dan, cut it out!" "Dan, if I can't expect you to play nicely with Caroline, I will take the blocks away!" Each time Laura yells from her desk and then goes back to her bills without checking on the children. The behavior stops briefly but inevitably, after a short while, resumes. Laura grows more and more tense and becomes increasingly disheartened about completing her task of doing the bills. Why can't Dan just do what he's told? After one particularly loud exchange in which Caroline begins to cry, Laura gets up from her chair, marches into the foyer, and screams, "OKAY! THAT'S IT! Those blocks are MINE! Dan, go to your room. Caroline, time for a nap!" Laura still feels tense and wants to lash out. Now both kids are upset; Caroline whimpers. Dan storms upstairs, slams his door shut, and yells, "You don't care about me at all! All you care about is doing your stupid bills!" His voice quavers through the shut door. Laura's mind kicks into high gear: Now look what I've gone and done. What an idiot. Some parent I am. I'll never get these stupid bills done now, and the kids just hate me.

After getting Caroline down for her nap, Laura is too upset herself to go back to her bills. What had gone so wrong? She feels like every time she tries to discipline the kids, whatever she tries makes the situation worse.

Getting Back on Course

Had Laura slowed down, she might have been able to take a minute to imagine how her actions might have felt for her *before* enacting them. Did they feel vital? She might have also been able to tell if they were consistent with her values of guiding her children well and spending quality time with them. Take a few moments now to reflect on Laura's experience.

EXERCISE: Reflecting on Laura's Experience

Take a few moments and write down ideas about what Laura might have done differently that might be consistent with her stated values:

- "Providing guidance for my children so that they grow up to be mature, loving adults"

- "Being with my children and enjoying them when they are young"

When Values Conflict (Revisited)

As we've mentioned, values in different areas of life sometimes conflict. In Laura's situation, her parenting values may have conflicted with her value to be financially responsible. A way to address this conflict is to notice in a given context what might be the best strategy—or at least the most effective one—given the situational constraints. If her value of being financially responsible had been her most important value that evening, Laura might have chosen to let the children argue it out and simply closed her door so she could focus on bills. Alternatively, Laura might have decided to simply sit down and build the castle with her children so that she might model things like taking turns, or she might have simply reveled in their presence. Of course, the cost of that would be staying up later to pay the bills or mailing them in late. Either way, there's a choice and a consequence; however, as mentioned before, these efforts may be balanced out over time.

The Course Is Not Always Straight

Parents are human too. Thus, you'll fall off the valued course at some point or another. Sometimes it's hard to tell when this happens, because some "falls" are fairly subtle. When you do discover that you are "in the weeds," as they say, your mind will likely kick in and tell you that it was a doomed endeavor anyway. Your mind is just trying to keep you safe by minimizing your errant ways. To return to our horizon metaphor, the winds blow you off course and the clouds of your mind start to roll in. And that's okay—your mind is just doing its job, which, simply put, is the minimization of risk. Just notice your mind's whispers—or shouts, as the case may be—and notice what you're doing about it: Have you come to a full stop on your valued course? Have you turned in the opposite direction? Notice how what you're doing feels to you.

As soon as you notice you've gone off course, you'll have another choice to make: will you return to your chosen course, or will you keep going in your new direction? Pursuing your values is not always a straightforward process. You'll probably make many missteps, especially when your child's behavioral challenges arise. It's important to remember that. It's also important to remember that your course is your own, and it's always up to you. There may be times that it feels vital to choose a new direction. It'll be important to consider the long-term, bigger picture rather than just to respond to your thoughts and feelings or what's easiest in the moment. It may also be important, if you are coparenting, to ask your partner about his or her wishes and to incorporate both parents' values in a way that looks and feels consistent to your child.

A Few Words on Values and Parent Training Programs

When you're deeply engaged in a struggle with your child's behavior, you may go to a psychologist, parenting classes, or a parent training clinic. One of the first things you'll be asked is what your goals are for treatment. As we mentioned before, values are not goals; if valuing is a direction, goals are the mileposts along that road. Sometimes it can be disheartening to focus exclusively on goals like increasing compliance or reducing aggression without remembering the bigger picture. Similarly the techniques that we know work well with children are often very simple in theory but difficult in practice. Also, it's often most critical to use those techniques in situations that you find the most challenging or when you're feeling your most vulnerable. When parents come to us with extremely difficult struggles with their children, they often see their children as simply problems to be solved. Keeping your values near to your heart, especially when seeking treatment or learning to correctly implement new parenting skills, can be very helpful. It can also dignify your struggle, because it places the hard work of parenting in the context of a greater purpose than simply fixing your child's problem behaviors.

Summary

Hopefully this chapter helped you clarify your values so that you can keep them close to your heart when you're in the thick of parenting. We also hope that now you have some ideas about how thoughts and feelings might keep you from parenting in a value-consistent way. In the next chapter, we'll discuss such difficulties and introduce some ways of dealing with them.

CHAPTER 4

Is the Goal Control?

Managing Feelings vs. Managing Behavior

Making the decision to have a child is momentous. It is to decide forever to have your heart go walking around outside your body.

Elizabeth Stone

A failure is not always a mistake, it may simply be the best one can do under the circumstances. The real mistake is to stop trying.

B. F. Skinner

Early childhood is a developmental period full of opportunities for you to guide your child's behavior. This time in your child's life requires you, in fact, to provide many rules and regulations. If you did not tell your child what and how much to eat, tell her when to sleep, and help her to avoid dangerous situations, for example, that would constitute neglect. You may have many strategies for guiding your child's behavior. Some of the strategies are probably effective in addressing the issues, and some are less so. Additionally, some strategies likely work very well in the short run, but you may notice yourself having to use these strategies again and again for the same or similar behaviors, which indicates they aren't very effective in the long run. Finally, you may find yourself using strategies inconsistently or quickly shifting from one to the next if what you're doing in a particular moment doesn't seem to be working. We believe that there's a common thread here that ties these ineffective strategies together in how they're used and in how they work. That common thread is *parenting to control your emotions rather than to help your child to behave well.*

As the parent of a young child, you'll often find yourself in situations in which you'll experience discomfort. Your child's tantrums, argumentativeness, or refusal to follow directions may distress you. Learning tasks or taking part in social situations that are challenging for your child may challenge you as well. You may also feel highly uncomfortable when you witness your child's distress, such as when he experiences intense anger, fear, sadness, embarrassment, or disappointment. In situations like these, you may attempt to control or change how you or your child feels rather than addressing your child's behavior; you may not even realize that this *emotion control* is happening and, when it happens, what the effects are for both you and your child.

In this chapter, we'll first offer you a new way of understanding your child's behavior as well as your own. Then we'll show you that the goal of emotion control —whether for yourself or your child—may prevent you from effectively and sensitively handling your child's behavior. We'll address how—and how well—these emotion control strategies work, and what they work for. We'll help you make a distinction between what *is* and what *is not* under your control and set the stage for learning strategies that can make a real difference in your relationship with and guidance of your young child.

Identifying the Why of Your Parenting: The Tool of Functional Analysis

Why do you do what you do as a parent? Sometimes you might explain this by looking at your own past history, or how you were parented. But there is a much simpler and more effective way to think about *why* you behave in certain ways around your children. To understand your parenting, we'll give you a tool called "functional analysis" that will help you look at how you parent somewhat differently than you might have in the past. Don't let the term "functional analysis" put you off, however. It's really as simple as learning your ABCs. It's also the cornerstone of extensively researched behavioral parenting strategies and, if used correctly, has been shown to work very well in helping parents understand their children's behavioral difficulties. In short, it's a way of thinking about how you or your child (or anyone, for that matter) behaves.

Functional analysis is a way of looking at how your behavior works for you (or how your child's behavior works for her). It's based on the idea that all behavior is connected to events that happen before and trigger it—we call these *antecedents*—and what happens after the behavior occurs—we call these *consequences*. All three components—antecedents, behavior, and consequences, or what we and others call the "ABCs"—are more or less likely to occur together in particular *contexts*—that is, in certain situations. For example, if you hear your doorbell (antecedent), this triggers your getting up to answer it (behavior). If you're annoyed that the person at the door is a traveling salesman (antecedent—A), you might politely send him away (behavior—B), thus reducing your annoyance (consequence—C). Your desire to send away the salesman might be particularly intense if you have a pot about to boil over on the stove and less pressing if you're bored and have nothing to occupy you (context). Let's take a closer look at the ABCs—antecedents, behavior, consequences—along with the concept of "context" in terms of your parenting.

Antecedents. When you're working to figure out the "what for" of a behavior, it's important to identify triggers, or antecedents. The way to do this is to ask yourself the question "What happened just before I did X?" Pretty much anything can be an antecedent: a particular situation, your child's behavior, or your child's expression of emotion, as well as your own thoughts, feelings, and physical sensations. Sometimes several of these things together create the antecedent or trigger. Antecedents get their power over your behavior from your life experiences, memories, meanings you give them, and how you feel about them. People learn from their own experiences and from watching or even hearing about the experiences of others. Whether, how quickly, and how well you learn depends on the context in which the learning happens.

Behavior. We think of behavior as actions. But behavior also includes thoughts and feelings and how you express them. *Behavior* is what you do, say, think, and feel. It can be observable by others—or, in the case of your own thoughts and feelings, just by you. Behavior is triggered by antecedents and is either encouraged or discouraged by its consequences.

Consequences. Consequences, simply stated, are the "results" of a particular behavior. For example, when you turn a faucet off, the consequence is that the water stops. Consequences, like antecedents, can also be many and varied. They include situations, the actions of others, your own feelings, and many other things. When your behavior directly results in a desirable consequence, you will likely engage in this behavior more often or with greater intensity. The things you want can vary: to get something or to get rid of something, to make something happen or to stop it or prevent it from happening. For example, if you're hungry, you might want to get a cookie, but if you're hurting from a rock in your shoe, you might do something to get rid of the rock.

Context. Context can mean many things. We could define it as the physical environment. But that's not all it is. Context includes the *meaning* that you give to particular events as well as your thoughts and feelings about those events.

Even if you understand the ABCs of your actions, you can't fully explain them unless you consider the context in which they occur. For example, you might not consider it a big deal if your child misbehaves in the privacy of your home (a private context), although it might be a very big deal if he does so in public (a public context). Similarly you may feel more challenged when your child defies you after a long and difficult day at work (context: you're feeling vulnerable) than on a leisurely Saturday afternoon when you're reminiscing about an enjoyable dinner with friends (context: you're relaxed and comfortable). Your child might do the same thing on either occasion, and because of the context, you might respond in a completely different way each time. Thus, context is an extremely important part of why and how you might choose your parenting or child-management strategies.

For a visual description of antecedents, behavior, consequences, and how all of these work within a context, see the diagram below.

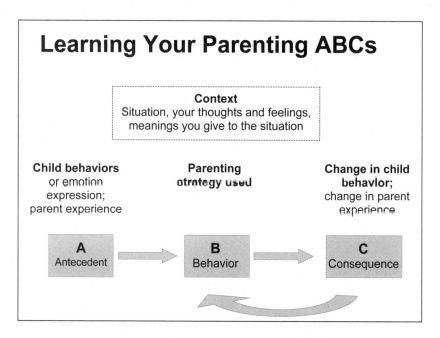

Learning Your Parenting ABCs

Context
Situation, your thoughts and feelings,
meanings you give to the situation

Child behaviors
or emotion
expression;
parent experience

Parenting
strategy used

**Change in child
behavior;**
change in parent
experience

A
Antecedent

B
Behavior

C
Consequence

As you can see in our diagram, your parenting behavior (or strategies) results in consequences both for your child and for you. There are two major kinds of consequences: these are called "reinforcers" and "punishers." *Reinforcers* are consequences that end up causing a behavior to happen more frequently. *Punishers* are consequences that result in a behavior occurring less frequently. Context determines the strength of the relationships between the ABCs and helps to give reinforcers and punishers their respective power.

Here's an exercise to help you understand why you parent as you do in particular contexts. It will also help you begin to understand the relationship between your thoughts and feelings and your parenting behaviors. You can use this exercise to walk through what your parenting strategies *do* for your child and for you.

EXERCISE: Your Core Strategies for Common Behavior Problems

In this exercise, you'll conduct a rough functional analysis of your parenting behavior. To help you do this, we've chosen some parenting situations that most, if not all, parents experience with their young child. We'd like for you to pay special attention to your thoughts and feelings as they might occur in the situations described below. After reading each of the questions, write your answer in your journal.

Your child throws a tantrum because you have made a demand. She is getting louder and more insistent.

- Identify the context: Where are you, and what is going on around you when your child begins the tantrum?

- Identify the antecedents: What are your thoughts and feelings while your child is having the tantrum? How does your body feel?

- Identify your behavior: How do you respond? What do you typically do to address the tantrum? Be as specific as possible.

- Identify the consequences for your child: What happens to your child's behavior?

- Identify the consequences for you: Immediately after you use this tactic, what happens to your thoughts and feelings? Do they change? Would you describe yourself as feeling better or worse?

Now try this one:

Your child resists going to bed by whining and crying, repeatedly asking for things like a drink or a snack, and telling you he's feeling very scared.

- Identify the context: What is going on for you in your own nighttime routine when your child begins resisting bedtime?

- Identify the antecedents: What are your thoughts and feelings while your child resists bedtime? How does your body feel?

- Identify your behavior: How do you respond? What do you typically do to address the resistance? Be as specific as possible.

- Identify the consequences for your child: What happens to your child's behavior?

- Identify the consequences for you: Immediately after you use this tactic, what happens to your thoughts and feelings? Do they change? Would you describe yourself as feeling better or worse?

What was it like for you to complete these exercises? Did you notice any patterns in your thoughts and emotions before or after you chose a particular parenting strategy? Note your reactions. You may have discovered that when you respond to your child, there are consequences for you as well as for her. You may have also noticed that your thoughts and emotions were sometimes antecedents to your responses to your child—and sometimes they may have been consequences. It's important to notice both. Now that you have some basic experience with using functional analysis and have used it to look at your own behavior in its context, let's use those skills to look a bit further at what you're parenting *for* and whether you're choosing the goal of emotion control.

What Are You Parenting For?

Parenting isn't always pleasant; at times, it is very hard. All parents, at least sometimes, feel stressed out by their children or feel impatient, angry, frustrated, or disappointed. Sometimes, such as when your child shows really strong emotions or behaves badly (for example, blowing up or lashing out), it can be extremely upsetting. In those moments, you may wish that you could make your child stop feeling what she's feeling. You might have thoughts like: *Why is she so afraid of everything? If he could just stop doing that. Oh no, here comes a tantrum. Why can't he just listen the first time? She's such a drama queen!* As we've mentioned before, many parents feel that when their children struggle with emotions or misbehave, it's a reflection of their bad parenting. When you struggle with these thoughts and feelings, it may become more important to you in that moment to manage your own feelings than to focus on what's best for your child. Thus, the choices you make about parenting strategies may be more about *you* and how *you* are thinking and feeling, and less about your *child.* Consider the following example.

✤ The First Day of Kindergarten

Katie and her mother, Susan, stand in the doorway of the kindergarten classroom. It's Katie's first day at school. Katie clings to her mother's leg, standing a little behind her. The room is bright and loud, and children are talking and laughing in the various play centers about the room. Susan feels Katie's grip tighten on her leg and hears her small, quavering voice say, "Mom, please don't make me go. Please. I'm scared." Susan leans down to soothe her. "It will be okay, Katie. Let's go in for a bit and see how it goes." Katie backs away from the door and says more loudly this time, "No! I don't want to. Let's just go home. I want to stay with you." Her eyes tear up. "This must be Katie," a teacher, who has just approached, says. "Why don't you let me show you some of our play centers and introduce you to your new friends?" Katie has gone pale. Her chest heaves and her shoulders are hunched. She doesn't speak to the teacher but instead stands behind Susan and holds on for dear life. "C'mon, Katie. Let's try it," urges Susan. "NO, NO, NO!" says Katie through her tears. She tries to pull Susan back into the hallway even as Susan tries to soothe her and convince her to enter the classroom. After a few minutes that seem like an eternity, Susan's chest begins to tighten and her pulse races. She feels as if she has to escape, just as Katie does. "She's just not ready. We'll try tomorrow," Susan states quietly to the teacher. "But," the teacher starts, "many children react this way the first day, and ..." "No," Susan replies. "It's not okay for her to be this upset." She scoops Katie up and makes for the door. "We're leaving, honey. It's going to be okay."

If we look at this story in terms of antecedents, behaviors, and consequences, Katie expressed her anxiety to Susan (antecedent), and Susan's response (behavior) was to take Katie home (consequence). For Katie, the immediate psychological consequence of Susan's response was that she probably felt much less distressed—and very likely so did Susan. However, there's a bit more to it than that if you consider the long-term consequences for both Katie and Susan.

What was Susan, Katie's mom, working *for* in this situation? Clearly, Susan tried to protect Katie from perceived harm—in particular, from feeling frightened and perhaps from being angry with or blaming Susan for taking her to the kindergarten class. In short, Susan was working for emotion control, or making her own discomfort—as well as that of her daughter—go away. On the face of it, that might appear to be consistent with values that all parents hold: to keep their children safe. After all, who wouldn't want to minimize a child's distress and fear or help her to avoid situations that might be uncomfortable or painful? Susan's experience was pretty stressful for her too. By letting her daughter escape from feeling anxious and scared, she also protected herself from her own discomfort in experiencing her daughter's anxiety. In the short run, this emotion control strategy may seem like a great idea.

Sometimes strategies that work very well in the short run, however, have unintended negative consequences in the long run. Because the contingencies of the present moment can be so potent and compelling, it's often hard to step back from how we react to things in an immediate way and look into the future. Yet there are good reasons why such short-term emotion control strategies backfire and may contribute to the development of more long-standing behavioral problems in children. Because Susan was unwilling to experience discomfort, Katie wasn't able to experience a potentially lovely day in the classroom. Moreover, Susan's behavior may have inadvertently taught Katie that the classroom was a place to be feared. That might make Katie feel even more frightened in the long run and prevent her from learning and using effective coping skills. Finally, Susan may have underestimated Katie's ability to cope with her fear. Thus, this parenting choice led to a lost opportunity for both Susan and her daughter and perhaps to greater difficulties down the road.

What might Susan have done differently? She might have encouraged Katie to stay. How she might have accomplished this in an ACT-consistent way will be addressed in chapter 9. For right now, the take-home message is twofold: first, notice when you might be relying on emotion control in your parenting strategies; second, understand the unintended, and often negative, consequences of this. In the next sections, we'll discuss three fairly typical emotion control strategies parents sometimes fall into in challenging situations like the one described above: giving in, getting loud, or giving up.

Common Control Strategies: Giving In, Getting Loud, or Giving Up

If your young child's behavior challenges you and you then resort to emotion control strategies, you may typically choose one of these three: "giving in," "getting loud," or "giving up." These strategies are usually very effective in changing your child's behavior in the short run but may cause problems in the long run. Some parents fall into these strategies when their children behave in a stubborn or argumentative way. Other parents resort to them when their children who are fearful refuse to follow rules because they're feeling afraid.

In the example story, Susan gave in to Katie's fearfulness. *Giving in* is—in the short run—a common, extremely effective strategy for stopping tantrums as well as for dealing with a child who clings to a parent at bedtime or school drop-off. Giving in may also involve asking or directing your child to do as you ask but then not following through on your demand. In the case of your child's difficulty separating from you, giving in may manifest itself as your lingering in the classroom or granting your child's request and taking her home. In other words, you may be too permissive or "hands-off," especially when you experience negative feelings arising from your child's negative feelings. However, as you have seen, giving in has unintended and even harmful effects in the long run. In fact, experts have found that giving in, or overly permissive parenting, is linked with more persistent child misbehavior—in particular, continued stubbornness, argumentativeness, and sometimes aggression.

In other situations, you may do just the opposite of giving in and instead *get loud*: you might escalate your demand, raise your voice, or assert more power. Parents who fall into this control strategy often become very harsh and punitive with their children. Some typical antecedents to getting loud include your experience of intense negative feelings like fear or anger. Your escalation will often stop your child's misbehaviors in the short run. However, this strategy, too, can backfire, and it has been linked with persistent child behavior problems.

The third common control strategy is *giving up*. It usually starts with parents saying, "I already tried that..." Sometimes parents who have gone through behavioral parent training programs or who have spoken with psychologists regarding their children's misbehavior feel that tried-and-true techniques just don't work. Thus, these parents try a string of different strategies, often switching from one to another in an unsystematic way. In short, they give up on a particular strategy and parent inconsistently. Often these parents are correct when they say that their strategies don't work, although the lack of effectiveness doesn't happen for the reasons they think. For example, when you learn an effective parenting strategy (as you will in chapters 6, 7, 8, and 9) but you don't use it consistently, your strategy will no longer be effective. Antecedents to using parenting strategies inconsistently include your child *upping the ante*, or misbehaving in a more intense, unpleasant way. And, of course, this might upset you or trigger negative self-evaluations of your parenting. When this happens, you might give up on the particular strategy you're using rather than stick to it.

To summarize, the control strategies of giving in, getting loud, and giving up work well in the short run. Specifically they tend to stop your child's misbehavior and, in so doing, stop you from feeling upset, frustration, or other negative emotions. When your behavior leads to your *feeling better*, we call this *negative reinforcement:* your reward is a sense of relief and the short-term banishment of feeling badly. However, in the long run, all of these strategies are ineffective in helping your child learn more appropriate behavior.

Controlling Emotions vs. Effectively Managing Behavior: Which Works Best?

Please understand that situations like those described above happen to all parents. There is no cure for occasional negative interactions with your child that result in unpleasant emotions and thoughts for you. Like most parents, you're probably uncomfortable in situations like the ones we described. You may feel tense or angry. You may feel irritated or anxious— those are antecedents for your behavior—or you may hear your mind chanting about how you are ineffective or incompetent. These experiences are very common, normally occur in the context of difficult child behavior, and are very powerful motivators of parenting behavior.

When children stop misbehaving, parents tend to feel relief and a reduction in tension, stress, anger, or anxiety. Those feelings act as the immediate consequence that keeps you choosing these control strategies. Because giving in, getting loud, and giving up are so effective or immediately rewarding, they have a very powerful influence over your behavior, especially in particularly challenging contexts. If it's more important to you in the moment to stop feeling uncomfortable about or embarrassed by your child's misbehavior, it will likely be hard for you to consistently use effective parenting strategies, since these often work over time rather than in the short run. So a good question to keep in mind as you choose your parenting strategies is this: *Is what I'm doing in this moment more about making me feel better, or is it in the best interest of my child in the long run?*

Parenting as Experiential Avoidance

There's a name for the emotion control strategies we've been discussing. As you may recall, when you're unwilling to experience psychological discomfort or distress, and you make strong and deliberate efforts to avoid, stop, minimize or otherwise control that distress, this is called experiential avoidance. Experiential avoidance may take many forms, and the form is often dependent on the particular context in which it occurs. We've already discussed how some parenting strategies—giving in, getting loud, and giving up—may be linked with experiential avoidance. Other common examples of experiential avoidance of thoughts, feelings, and bodily sensations are these:

- Trying not to think about something when it "shows up" in your thoughts

- Arguing with your mind

- Distracting yourself from your thoughts or feelings

- "Getting busy" rather than thinking about things

- Avoiding situations in which unwanted feelings or thoughts arise

- Avoiding or escaping being with individuals around whom such experiences tend to happen

- Avoiding behavior that may bring up painful thoughts or feelings

- "Tuning out" through watching TV or engaging in another activity that prevents you from thinking

- "Overanalyzing" thoughts and emotions

You may have noticed that some strategies mentioned in this list are almost opposites—for example, "tuning out" suggests "getting numb" or not thinking about anything at all and "overanalyzing" means being too much in your head. Well, you're right—these things do appear to be opposites on the surface, but in function they're the same: both tuning out and overanalyzing reflect attempts to modify or control your thoughts, feelings, and other experiences.

You might do whatever you can in the moment to *stop* situations that make you feel bad. The following exercise will help you contact some of your feelings and thoughts as they arise in parenting situations and give you a sense of experiential avoidance.

EXERCISE: Clouds on Your Horizon

Remember the desert island metaphor for parenting that we presented in chapter 3? Well, once you're ready to head off in a valued direction, sometimes clouds come into your view and block your horizon. Sometimes clouds are white and fluffy; they seem light. Other times, they're dark and full of doom. Take a minute to reflect on what you think and how you feel about the two different kinds of clouds. Then consider that all clouds do eventually float by—that's what clouds do.

Now, using the clouds as symbols for your experiences of parenting, continue with the exercise:

Imagine yourself, if you can, sailing toward your horizon—to what you want for yourself and for your child. See yourself in your boat, with your buoys floating behind you, heading to the sunrise and feeling the warmth of the sun.

Now imagine that a white, fluffy cloud floats by. Think of a word or a snapshot that captures a moment when you felt really good about your child or your parenting. Place that word or snapshot on the cloud. (If you can't do this, that's okay—just notice that.) As you think about that moment, notice what you feel in your body, what you think, and how you feel. Now put those bodily sensations, thoughts, and feelings on their own white clouds—and watch all the clouds float by. Notice how quickly or slowly they move. Notice what direction they came from and where they're going. Pay attention to what you want to happen with them—what you want to do with sensations, thoughts, and feelings. And let them just drift away so you can once again see your horizon clearly. Sail on as the clouds drift away.

Imagine that, unexpectedly, a dark, threatening cloud appears on the horizon. Think of a word or a snapshot that captures a moment when you felt badly about your child or your parenting. Place that word or snapshot on the cloud. (If you can't do this, that's okay. Just notice that.) As you think about that moment, notice what you feel in your body, what you think, and how you feel. Now put those bodily sensations, thoughts, and feelings on their own dark clouds—and watch all of the clouds float by. Notice how quickly or slowly they move. Notice what direction they came from and where they're going. Pay attention to what you want to happen with them—what you want to do with these thoughts, sensations, and feelings.

Take a few moments to write in your journal about your experience of this exercise. If you have thoughts like This is silly, This is stupid, or I can't do this, just write them down. If you can, write about how you responded to your thoughts and feelings on the clouds. Pay attention to whether or not your responses differed for the clouds attached to dark thoughts and feelings versus those associated with light, peaceful thoughts and feelings. And pay attention to how your responses affected your view of the horizon and your movement toward it. What happened when you let the clouds simply drift? What happened when you tried not to think about them?

You may notice that you responded somewhat differently to the white and dark clouds. It's sometimes easier to observe experiences that are perceived as pleasant without reacting to them than it is unpleasant or unwanted experiences. You may also have noticed that the clouds behaved differently when you just let them drift on versus when you tried not to think about them. Unfortunately, attempts to ignore them can often make those unwanted experiences stick around and turn you away from your valued direction. Reflect on how you experienced the cloud exercise and see if that wasn't so for you. If it was, you have come in contact with why trying to manage your thoughts and feelings doesn't work. Trying to push away your feelings in parenting situations works much the same way as trying to push away those dark clouds in the previous exercise: it gets in the way of your focusing on what's best for your child. In other words, trying to control how you feel and think (or how your child feels and thinks) is often an *unworkable* strategy. It just doesn't work the way you might want it to work.

Considering the Context: When the Volume Goes Up in Your Mind

We spent some time discussing antecedents that sometimes trigger emotion control strategies. What's going on for you in a particular moment can also influence whether you choose an emotion control strategy—or whether you stay focused on your child's best interests. Situations in which your child misbehaves can be particularly evocative of experiential avoidance. This might be even more problematic when those situations are in public (for example, at the mall) rather than in private (for example, in your own home). Consider Tyrell's story as an example.

❧ On Display

Tyrell is three and a half, and a bright, boisterous child. He asks his mother, Jill, to get him a large toy robot at a local department store. She is on a tight budget and says no. He begins to whine and cry, and Jill is overtaken by a familiar tension and feeling of stress. As he cries louder and louder, she's flooded with negative thoughts about herself (Everybody's looking at me; I'm a terrible parent) and about Tyrell (He's such a brat!). She feels angry and embarrassed, and her heart rate shoots through the roof. People stare, and she can only imagine what they're thinking. Suddenly it's as if she can't think—she has no idea what to do. One woman gives her a long, unfriendly look and walks away. "Okay, okay, Tyrell," she says. "You can have it. Just ssshhh!"

You might recognize the control strategy of giving in here. If Tyrell had behaved similarly at home—for example, asking for a cookie that she didn't have—it would have been easier for Jill to stand firm and say "No." She might also have felt less vulnerable. However, being in public and experiencing Tyrell throw a fit was pretty embarrassing for Jill. Thus, she tried to end her discomfort by giving in to Tyrell. What's more, because she was so focused on her own thoughts and feelings, this short-circuited her ability to think carefully about what might have been a more effective parenting strategy for Tyrell in the long run. In short, she chose a knee-jerk response without considering the long-term consequences of her action: because Jill gave in, Tyrell will be much more likely to throw a tantrum in the future because this behavior got him what he wanted.

When you focus on avoiding unpleasant thoughts and feelings, you probably won't be able to think of a more adaptive and flexible way of coping with the immediate problem. This can potentially prevent you from learning more effective strategies of behavior management. If you can't think of or try other strategies, you might never have the opportunity to learn what works best in the long run. Complete the next exercise to help you understand what triggers and contexts evoke your use of emotion control strategies.

EXERCISE: Understanding Your Triggers and Contexts

1. Take a few minutes to consider typical interactions you have with your child that might be challenging for you and that might elicit negative thoughts and emotions. These might be times when your child refuses to follow your directions or ignores you, or perhaps they involve back talk or fearfulness.

2. Think about when these types of interactions are easy for you to handle. Write those situations in your journal.

3. Think about times when and places where these interactions are really difficult for you to handle or are particularly stressful for you. Remember, contexts can include where you are (private vs. public places) as well as how you're feeling (relaxed and comfortable vs. stressed, tired, and vulnerable). Write these down.

4. What contexts are difficult for you? What emotions/situations for you are particularly problematic? What emotions/situations with your child are particularly challenging? Do you notice any patterns in terms of your choice of parenting or control strategies? For example, in which situations are you more likely to give in, get loud, or give up? Notice these, and write down your observations.

When you've finished the exercise, give yourself a pat on the back: you have successfully accomplished what many parents can't. You've begun to look at your parenting differently and are increasing your awareness of when you're using emotion control strategies. That's really hard to do! Noticing and stopping these strategies are the first steps toward learning new, more effective parenting strategies, which we will teach you in chapters 6, 7, 8, and 9.

If Emotion Control Strategies Don't Work, Then What?

So now you might be wondering, *If emotion control strategies don't work, then what do I do?* That's a very good question, and we'll answer it in the next chapter. In short, we'll suggest that what you do right now is change your strategy a bit. We'll suggest that, rather than try to manage and control your thoughts and feelings, you allow yourself to *experience* your thoughts and feelings—good or bad—when you're with your child. Doing this can free you up to really focus on being with your child. We'll teach you how to pay attention in an accepting manner to the present moment. This strategy is sometimes called "mindfulness," which we will discuss in detail in chapter 5. We'll show you that if you stop trying to control your feelings and simply observe what's happening in the present moment, you may be able to be a more responsive, sensitive, and effective parent.

Summary

In this chapter, we gave you the tool of functional analysis to help you think about what you're parenting *for* in particular situations and to identify the consequences of your actions for your child and yourself. We also discussed what happens when you try to manage your emotions rather than managing your child's behavior. Although they can seem helpful in the short run, attempts to parent in this way often backfire and lead to negative long-term consequences. Hopefully we've set the stage for you to begin learning about new ways to work toward your values as a parent in coming chapters. In the next chapter, we will teach you how to develop and use mindfulness skills to help you choose effective parenting strategies in difficult moments with your child.

CHAPTER 5

Being Mindful

Appreciating Your Child

The most precious gift we can offer others is our presence. When mindfulness embraces those we love, they will bloom like flowers.

Thich Nhat Hanh

Love isn't a state of perfect caring. It is an active noun like struggle. To love someone is to strive to accept that person exactly the way he or she is, right here and now.

Fred Rogers

Ever notice that when your child engages in an activity she loves—like playing pretend, blowing bubbles, or building a sand castle—she's completely present and focused on that one thing in the moment? You may have tried, with little success, to call her to dinner or attract her attention for some other purpose. Think about times when you're with your child—maybe he's playing tee ball or climbing on gymnastic equipment. His face is filled with joy. He's unconcerned with sadness or worry. Children having experiences like these may be directed, focused, playful, or all of these at the same time. In such a moment, their worries—if they have any—may be far off on the horizon, like dark clouds that are gently acknowledged and then pass, leaving little trace of their existence.

Can you remember the last time you felt like that, when you were entranced and fully focused on the things that were most important to you—when you fully appreciated them and noticed all of their facets without your mind getting *hooked* (caught up) on a thought or feeling that broke the spell?

Can you think of a time when—intentionally—you were able to pay attention in a particular way and to just notice the scene around you? Take a few minutes to do that now: just notice, without making any judgment about it, the experience of holding this book as you read it. What is the book's weight? What about its texture? Without reading the words, can you picture them laid out on the pages? What about the white spaces between the words and letters?

In a situation like this, there's probably little room for comparing this book with others, or rating its pages, or wishing for some different, better experience of just holding a book. You may—without resistance, evaluation, or reaction—very simply notice and appreciate all that is around you, for the sake of simply noticing. Now let your awareness gently expand: consider the reasons that you're reading this book and working through the exercises in it. Let yourself feel that there's something important in it for you, something about your parenting and about your relationship with your child. Just notice, without evaluating or trying to change anything, your feelings about that. It may be harder for you to simply notice this without reaction. This may take practice.

In this chapter, we'll teach you about "mindfulness," this skill of simple, purposeful "noticing" that you can develop over time. We'll show you how you can incorporate mindfulness in your relationship with your child—in joyful moments, in day-to-day interactions, and also in more difficult situations. In the ACT model, mindfulness includes a process called "defusion," which we briefly introduced in chapter 2. As you may recall, defusion helps you notice your thoughts and feelings for what they are—as changing events rather than permanent facts or literal truths. Learning defusion is a useful parenting skill, because when you're fused with your thoughts and feelings rather than having some distance from them, you're often taken away from what's actually going on around you in the present moment.

What Is Mindfulness?

What exactly is mindfulness? We use the term "to be mindful" in many situations. For example, we're "mindful" of the time or "mindful" of others' feelings or preferences. When we use this phrase, it typically means awareness and acknowledgment of something. Mindfulness, however, is much more than that. *Mindfulness* is a skill, cultivated through practice, of purposeful attention in a nondefensive, nonevaluative way. Although it's an idea very much in our cultural awareness today, it has its roots in Eastern philosophy and in a number of religions. Recently psychologists and researchers have begun to ask questions about the nature of mindfulness and how it might be useful with emotional issues such as anxiety and depression, stress, chronic health conditions, eating disorders and substance use. It's also been shown to be useful for parents who must cope with children who struggle with disabilities, such as autism and behavioral problems (Blackledge and Hayes 2006).

The research shows that parents who use mindfulness experience a reduction in stress, anxiety, and depression. Children of parents who are mindful have fewer problem behaviors and better social interactions (Singh et al. 2006). Similarly parents who are less likely to use mindfulness are more likely to use harsh, more punishing parenting strategies, especially when they're coping with a number of stressors (Shea and Coyne 2009). Therefore, mindfulness may be viewed as a pathway to better emotional health and better behavioral functioning.

While mindfulness is a relatively easy concept to grasp, it's not necessarily a simple phenomenon. It has four facets, however, that you may find helpful in your daily life. Ruth Baer and colleagues (2006) describe these facets as the abilities to

1. verbally describe your experience fully, including thoughts and emotions;

2. act with care and with full awareness of your experience;

3. fully have your own experience in a nonjudgmental way; and

4. experience your internal psychological state without reacting.

Although the ability to observe and be aware of your own internal experience is also a part of what is meant by mindfulness, it's easy to get caught up in your own thoughts while engaging in this type of self-observation, especially if you haven't had a lot of practice at being mindful. Experienced meditators are more able to self-monitor in an accepting, nondefensive way than people just learning mindfulness (Baer et al. 2006). So what does this mean for you as a parent? Well, for one thing, it means that by practicing mindfulness you may find that you're less stressed and more able to parent effectively.

Practicing Mindfulness as a Way of Being

You may be intimidated by mindfulness because you think it means that you have to sit on a cushion in a dark corner for hours at a time or retreat to a cave in the mountains. Meditation, however, is just one way to increase mindfulness. We'll offer a few exercises in this section that will help you cultivate mindfulness in your daily life without having to run away to the mountains. You can be mindful while washing the dishes, walking to work, playing with your children, or working at your desk. Mindfulness is a way to stay in contact, in an accepting way, with the present moment (Hayes and Wilson 2003). Staying in the present in this way—rather than getting pulled into the past or the future—brings you into contact with both external and internal events, which we briefly mentioned earlier in this book. *External* events refer to those things that are going on around you. *Internal* events include your thoughts, feelings, and bodily sensations. Noticing that there is a "self" that is present, a "you" who recognizes these events and is greater than their content, is an important skill. (This is called "self-as-context," and we'll explore this idea more fully below.) Yet, sometimes this is difficult to do. But please don't get discouraged; we'll help you learn this skill as we move through this chapter. Just hang in there with us!

As you begin to develop your own skill of mindful awareness, you'll likely notice shifts and changes in what you're focusing on and begin to recognize your awareness moving from internal and external events. Most often, you may find yourself getting "hooked" by certain thoughts or feelings that you perceive or evaluate as undesirable. For example, you may sit down to do a mindfulness exercise and within seconds a string of thoughts vie for your attention: *I need to do the laundry* or *I wonder if I can get off work in time to pick Jane up from school and get her to swim practice and still get home for dinner.* You might have the thought *I'm doing this wrong.* Mindfulness is, in a way, great for slowing down the ongoing, pervasive chatter of your mind. Here are some examples of things you might notice during mindfulness exercises:

■ Passing thoughts	■ Emotions
■ Perceptions	■ Evaluations
■ Expectations	■ Attributions
■ Opinions	■ Mental images
■ Gut feelings	■ Muscle tension
■ Breathing	■ Moods
■ Physical sensations	■ Lapses in concentration
■ Worries	■ Ideas
■ List-making	■ Reason-giving

When being mindful, notice these things without making any judgments about them. If the laundry pulls at your attention, just notice it as a thought, but don't let it pull you out of the present moment. Mindfulness doesn't *get rid* of your thoughts and feelings—instead it helps you fully experience them without responding to them. Sound hard? Remember, mindfulness doesn't often come easily to people. It's a skill that needs to be practiced over time. To help you develop that skill, we've included a series of exercises to help you experience different aspects of mindfulness. It's probably best if you try these when you have some quiet time to yourself—perhaps early in the morning or late in the evening when your child is asleep and you don't have competing demands on your time and attention.

Mindfulness as Description

Are you able to describe what's going on around you and inside you in words, or is it sometimes difficult to put things into words? Although you may be able to contact your experiences through images, memories, or physical sensations, bringing things into your awareness is often linked with verbal descriptions of them. In fact, as you well know, it's nearly impossible to turn off the verbal activity of your mind! However, one element of mindfulness is exactly that: noticing the richness of your own experience and putting that into words. Try the following five-minute exercise to help you notice, very broadly, the aspects of what may seem at first to be a simple, straightforward experience. Read through the exercise once so you can do it without referring to the book.

EXERCISE: Awareness of the Smallest Sound

Sit in a comfortable position. Place a timer or a clock near you and set it for five minutes. Either close your eyes or find a spot to focus on, such as a small area of the wall or floor.

Take a few breaths in and out at your regular pace. If you notice yourself trying to control your breath or feeling like you need to change it, simply let those efforts go. Your body has been breathing on its own all of your life and needs no extra help.

Listen for the smallest sound you can hear. You might hear your own breathing or your heart beating. There's no correct thing to hear; simply notice the quietest sound that you can make out. Focus on it for just a few short moments. Pay attention to the smallest sound and allow your awareness to settle on it.

When the five minutes is up, open your eyes or broaden your visual field.

Now, in your parenting journal, write down—in as much detail as possible—what you heard. Make sure to include what it was like hearing that small sound, whether it was easy or hard, and whether any thoughts or feelings were associated with the sound or with the process of hearing it. Write your description such that someone who didn't listen for the smallest sound could read your words and know what it was like to hear it.

Was there anything different about this experience of noticing compared with your experiences in the past? Did the level of detail that you noticed change in any way? Many times, mindful noticing entails richer, more sophisticated awareness and description of events.

Mindfulness as Purposeful Attention or Awareness

As you did the exercise above, you may have noticed that your mind wandered. Even in very brief mindfulness exercises, it's often hard to have a quiet mind. If your mind did wander, consider the following: did you notice the moment it veered up and out of the exercise, or was it already long gone when you first discovered that it had gone off course? The act of noticing that your mind gets off track, and bringing it back to the exercise at hand, is mindfulness. If you're like most people learning how to do mindfulness exercises or meditation, your mind was probably off on its own, daydreaming, list-making, or engaged in some other distraction before you caught it. Mindfulness, in part, as we have mentioned earlier, involves nurturing the skill of purposeful attention or awareness as a *choice*. This choice can be made no matter what you're doing—whether you're sitting quietly without distraction, or walking, or eating, or being in the center of a crowded room or with your child. Of course, it's easier to learn how to pay attention to your experience in quiet, relaxed situations than busy, loud ones. Nonetheless, try the next exercise to see what we mean about practicing mindfulness anywhere. Read through the exercise once so you can do it without referring to the book.

EXERCISE: Walking Meditation

Take about five minutes, or ten if you have it, and go for a walk. The walk can be inside or outside, and it can be at whatever pace that you choose. Know that you only have to pay attention to what the experience is like for you.

Before you begin your walk, allow your eyes to become relaxed: they should be open to guide your path but not staring.

As you walk, focus your awareness on the experience of walking: what it feels like to pick up your feet and to place them down, what the floor or ground feels like beneath you. Notice how your weight shifts, how your arms move or stay still by your side. See if your feet rock as you step, or if you can feel a difference in the ways that your hips point out or roll in, depending on your direction. Notice how the air feels on your skin, how it shifts around you as you move. Notice the things around you or in your path.

If your attention wavers or your thoughts get in the way of the experience, bring your attention back to your breathing as you move, and notice how your posture and breath are linked. Notice if the temperature of certain parts of your body is different from others as you move. Your only task is to be aware of your walking and how it relates to your senses and to your thoughts and feelings as you move in the moment.

Take a few moments to write down your experiences in your journal. What were your responses to this exercise? Were there parts you found difficult, parts that you found easy, or both?

Mindfulness Without Evaluation or Reaction

So now that you've tried your hand at a few mindfulness exercises, you may have noticed your mind telling you whether you're doing a good job—or not. Your mind may even go so far as to give you a list of evaluations: *these exercises are stupid, this is too hard,* or worse—*you're stupid, you lack skill, and you'll never get any better.* Wow! If you had a friend who said these things to you, would you remain friends? Probably not. At the very least, you'd probably defend yourself to your friend.

You can't get rid of your mind and its chatter. And you probably wouldn't want to—at least some of the time, these judgments help you. Your mind helps you stay safe and figure out the answers to many problems. It's unhelpful, though, if it relies too heavily on avoidance of your experiences as a coping strategy. In any case, what you may have noticed in these exercises is that a large percentage of that chatter is unpleasant. Your mind probably spends a lot of time evaluating how you go about your daily life, no matter what you're doing. Thus, one critical facet of mindfulness is to simply notice your thoughts as thoughts—and nothing more. Try this next exercise to get a sense of what we mean by that.

EXERCISE: Notice the Words

Read the sentence below and try to notice, just notice, the words on the page.

My child is perfect, and I am an extraordinary parent.

Now take a few minutes to write in your journal about your experience of reading that sentence. Were you able to notice, without judgment, the words presented to you? Note what thoughts and feelings, if any, came up when you read the sentence.

Most people who are new to mindfulness won't be able to just notice the words. In fact, it's common for people to react fairly strongly. Many times people who've just read a sentence like the one above, or had a thought similar to it, will find themselves having some mixture of experiences. Sometimes people experience relief or joy, while at the same time, or almost immediately thereafter, they feel saddened or angry. You may have noticed that your mind started arguing about the truth of the sentence. Notice now, in this moment, what you're thinking about that exercise.

Getting Hooked by Your Thoughts

Mindful awareness is sort of like casting a net into a stream: you'll catch some things that you want—things that are good or desirable. However, you'll also catch things you'd rather not have thought about, envisioned, or felt—things like your mind's negative evaluations of you, your competence, or what have you. Very often, these are the types of experiences that "hook" you and pull you out of the present and into the past or the future. This may be especially the case when you're in challenging contexts—for example, experiencing stress in or about your relationship or interactions with your child.

Try the exercise below to see what we mean. Do you remember in chapter 4 when we asked you to observe clouds drifting across your horizon and showed you different ways of noticing them? Now we're going to give you an opportunity to practice observing your thoughts and feelings about your child.

EXERCISE: Appreciating Your Child

Read through the exercise once or twice before you begin. Don't rush through—take your time with each step.

1. Sit quietly and pay attention to your breathing. Just let your breath pass in and out naturally.

2. Imagine a pleasant moment you have recently shared with your child. Do the best you can to really put yourself back in that situation. Try to bring back what you saw, heard, and even smelled. How does your body feel? What thoughts and feelings do you have about your child?

3. Notice your child's face and the look on her face. What do you see?

4. Whatever thoughts or feelings you have about this moment with your child, let them linger as long as they wish. See if you can notice these thoughts and feelings to the fullest extent. Maybe you notice them as bodily sensations, or perhaps your thoughts occur as pictures in your mind. Maybe you actually see the words. Whatever the case, simply notice, and let the thoughts and feelings linger or pass as they wish.

5. Now notice what you want to do with the thoughts and feelings: Do you want to make them stop or push them out of your view? Do you want to argue with them? How do you feel about them?

6. Think about your relationship with your child. Let whatever feelings you have about that show up. Something that shows up for many parents are evaluations of their child, their relationship with their child, or their own competence as a parent. For example, you might think *I am not patient enough with my child* or perhaps *I'm not sure I'm doing the best job in parenting her.* Whatever the thoughts and feelings are, whether they are positive or negative evaluations, simply let them come into your awareness and acknowledge them. Notice how many there are and how you feel about all of these feelings and thoughts.

7. Now see if you can simply sit with those emotions and thoughts as they slip into your awareness without doing anything but allowing them to be in your presence. If you notice the urge to hurry them along or make them stop, simply acknowledge that as well, and let it be within your awareness.

8. If you struggle to change or stop your thoughts and feelings about your child or your parenting, notice that you're slipping out of your mindful

awareness. Bid those thoughts and feelings to enter again into that awareness and to come and go as they wish.

What did you notice as you did this exercise? Was it difficult for you to bring your imagined moment with your child into the present? Did you feel taken out of this imagined present moment by any particular thought? Sometimes, even with practice, it's hard to stay in the present moment. Many things trigger your movement out of the present. For example, difficult thoughts may pass through your mind, you may feel bored, or you may experience external distractions like noise, an odd smell, or even changes in temperature or light. Just as soon as you become more fully aware of your thoughts and feelings, something might jolt you from that awareness. Consider what you have learned about your mind. Your mind makes all kinds of comparisons and judgments; it's very good at evaluation. Your mind can sometimes get in the way of your being the parent you want to be; sometimes your mind is simply a nuisance. There's something remarkable, though, about how our minds work. Even without directly experiencing some event, you can still learn about it. For example, you likely have never been hit by a train, but you know to stay away from oncoming trains so you don't get crushed.

A Few Words on the Literality of Thoughts

If you found the preceding exercise hard, you're not alone. In the ACT model, the primary goal of mindfulness is to remain in full contact with the stream of your internal and external experiences without any attempt to change them. However, some thoughts may create more of a tug on your attention than others. The reason for this is that you—and all humans—are verbal creatures. You use words and language to describe nearly everything. One really amazing thing that words allow you to do—which is something that animals without language probably can't—is to contemplate the future and mull over the past. Words allow you to evaluate and categorize things as past/present, good/bad, or large/small and to make any number of other comparisons. Your use of language allows you to bring your memories of the past and anticipation of the future into your present awareness. You (and all humans) tend to experience your thoughts and respond to them *literally*—that is, as though they were real or true. For example, if you think about sucking a lemon, you might find yourself salivating and puckering your lips. Or if you think about something frightening happening to you or someone you love, you might tense up. When this happens, you're responding to your thoughts as though they were real things. This is called *fusion* with your thoughts: in other words, you experience your thoughts as literal, actual truths. To explore the nature of this phenomenon, try the next exercise.

EXERCISE: Describing the Dibotoda

Please describe a "dibotoda" in careful detail, just as you described the experience of your smallest sound.

You're likely feeling confused right now. Just be aware of that feeling. Do you feel it anywhere in your body? What are you thinking? Are you reminded of anything?

Now suppose that I tell you that "dibotoda" is the word for "temper tantrum" in a foreign language. You can likely now describe a dibotoda in great detail. You can probably tell what it looks like, what it sounds like, how it makes you feel, and how you want to act in response to it. Go ahead and do that now. Write your description in your parenting journal.

Notice that there isn't an actual child having a tantrum or even a description of a child having a tantrum here on these pages; it's just the word itself—indeed, just a collection of letters that initially made no sense to you. Yet you can, and likely did—after we suggested that dibotoda meant "tantrum" in a foreign language—have a strong reaction. Perhaps you experienced some tension or had visions of your own or someone else's child having a tantrum. Note that even though you were simply describing a word, it elicited some of the actual feelings, thoughts, memories, or sensations that you might have if your child were actually throwing a tantrum. That is what is meant by experiencing your thoughts as literal, actual events.

Mindful Acceptance and Defusion

As you can see, words can stand in for experiences. The word "tantrum" can produce the actual feelings of frustration, anger, and impatience that an actual tantrum might have produced in you. Words standing for experiences is usually a great aid: it saves us time and allows us to learn without having to always directly experience things. For example, if you hear someone yell "Fire!" in a crowded room, you can safely escape without having to be burned or hurt by smoke inhalation, or even having to see flames or smell smoke. However, words also make temper tantrums (and all kinds of other negative things) present. And you really can't change that, at least not for very long.

You may wonder, then, what the point of mindfulness is, if it's not to bring about change in unwanted experiences and if, instead, it paradoxically brings you into greater contact with them! If the purpose of mindfulness isn't to change anything or to change your thoughts or experiences, then why do it?

To answer this question, let's return to some things we covered a while back. Earlier we described the nonjudgmental, nonevaluative nature of mindfulness. To be fully present to all aspects of your experience, whether internal or external, you must inherently be accepting of those experiences. When you're able to accept your experiences in that way and you're able to sustain that contact regardless of the content of your thoughts or the intensity of your emotions or bodily sensations, the *nature* of your experience changes. You begin to notice your thoughts for what they are: simply thoughts rather than literal truths. When you do this, you're less likely to get "hooked" because your thoughts lose their power over your behaviors. Consider the following example.

❧ *The Just-So Pizza*

Ruth, a single mother, has attended individual parent training sessions for help with her child, George, for several weeks. George is four years old and often tries to bully his mother to get what he wants—typically through yelling at her, whining, or throwing a tantrum in protest when she sets limits or gives him a direction. Ruth has learned a number of useful skills: how to give directions clearly and simply, to be consistent, and to selectively attend to George's good behavior and to ignore the bad. She also understands that George has to learn not simply to stop these behaviors but also to find more appropriate ways of expressing himself. However, it's very hard for her to use these skills in public—for example, in restaurants. Last week she and George went out for pizza at a local joint. She allowed George to choose the type of pizza, and when it arrived she cut him a piece and put it on his plate. When he tried unsuccessfully to pick it up, he screamed and cried and refused to eat. At the time, Ruth lost her temper and yelled back at him: "You chose it, you have to eat it, and that's that!" George's screaming worsened to the point that Ruth grabbed his hand and led him out of the restaurant. She felt embarrassed, worried what the other restaurant patrons thought, and had imagined smacking her son on the bottom for his bad behavior. Her mind told her, You are a complete failure as a parent. What's more, everyone knows it. She immediately flushed and hurried faster down the street, away from the restaurant. She felt utterly exhausted and demoralized, and she desperately wanted to take a vacation far from her son, his bad behavior, her own responsibilities, and her mind's constant battering.

After a number of mindfulness training sessions in which Ruth practiced—in therapy and out—her mindfulness skills, especially in the context of her interactions with her child, she gained some distance from her self-evaluative thoughts. She still had them; she actually noticed more of them than before, but somehow they didn't mean the same thing to her. They didn't grab her or pull her into an argument with her mind the way they did before. They came and went like passing clouds.

So Ruth decided to test her mindfulness skills during a foray with George back to the same pizza joint. Once again, she let George choose what pizza to order. She noticed how sure he was of what he wanted, the way he smiled and looked at her gratefully, and how he beamed with pride when she let him place the order as well. She noticed her mind saying things to her like Wow, when he throws a tantrum again, this restaurant will ask us to never come back and You couldn't handle it before, what makes you think anything will be different now? These thoughts were still attached to strong feelings of fear, dread, and the mental image of Ruth ducking quickly out of the restaurant. However, she sat with them and simply noticed what it was like to have such thoughts—their weight, their tug on her attention, and how they passed when she gently drew her focus back to George. Despite feeling tense in her chest and shoulders and fearful that a tantrum was inevitable, George's playful antics made her smile. She remembered when he was smaller and how he always wanted things "just so." An idea shone in her mind. "George," she said, "what was it that you didn't like about the pizza here the last time? You just ordered the same one as before." George stopped playing with his fork and furrowed his brow. "When I tried to pick it up, it was floppy, and the juice dripped in my sleeve. It felt really gross and burned a little 'cause it was really hot," he replied. "Oh," she said. "Let's see if we can wait a bit before we eat it this time to see if it cools off and gets a bit less floppy. That a good idea?" "Yes!" said George happily. When the pizza arrived, Ruth distracted George for a few minutes by playing a game and pointing out different pictures on the wall. When they began eating, the pizza was cool and crisp, and George ate a slice and a half, with gusto.

Ruth's mindfulness skills paid off—she was able to notice more than just the negative aspects of her experience. When she opened herself more broadly to the experience of getting pizza with George and managed to avoid getting "hooked" by troublesome thoughts, she was able to address the situation in a way that hadn't occurred to her before. When Ruth welcomed all aspects of her experience, new ideas showed up.

Self-as-Context: Defusion and You as an Observer

When you practice mindfulness consistently, you'll notice quite clearly that you aren't the sum total of your thoughts, emotions, and bodily responses. This is the *self-as-context* concept that we briefly mentioned earlier in this chapter: there's a *you* that's doing the observing. When you're fused with your thoughts and emotions, you aren't aware of the "observer you." However, when you practice mindful awareness, your thoughts and emotions are more like scenes being played out—you can welcome and acknowledge them, then let them pass. The "you" doing the observing is stable, rooted, and unchanging. It's this "you" that chooses how you experience your thoughts—as literal truths or as inevitable, ever-changing mental activity.

One way to help make the distinction between your thoughts and the "you" who experiences those thoughts is to imagine a chessboard (Hayes, Strosahl, and Wilson 1999). You—or, more specifically, the observer you—are the chessboard. The black pieces are your unwanted thoughts and emotions. The white pieces are your mind's defense system as it becomes engaged in argument with these thoughts and emotions and strives to refute them. When you are fused with your thoughts—in other words, when you feel they're true and are the sum total of who you are—you're up on the board in the middle of the battle between the pieces. When you engage in mindfulness practice and become defused from your thoughts, you are the board—stable, unchanging, watching the battle from a distance, and experiencing it for what it is: your mind's endless, perhaps unpleasant but harmless activity rather than a representation of yourself.

Defusion and Psychological Flexibility

As you grow more comfortable with mindfulness skills, you may notice that, rather than your familiar avoidance strategies arising (for example, in Ruth's case, simply cooping the situation), a broader set of choices may arise. And, as we know, there can be great freedom in choice. In chapter 4, we discussed the skill of functional analysis—that is, noticing what leads up to a behavior and what actions (or consequences) serve to maintain the behavior. After some practice with mindfulness, Ruth was better able to assess what had led to George's misbehavior, learn from that, and change her strategy so that it didn't become problematic during their second trip to the pizza place.

The broadened awareness of and ability to effectively act on choices is often referred to as *psychological flexibility* (Wilson and Murrell 2004). When you're fused with unwanted thoughts or feelings, your behavior often focuses on one thing only: to minimize or stop that experience, whether through suppressing your thoughts or feelings or actually physically avoiding or escaping external events that trigger it. In either case, you'll probably remember (see chapters 1 and 4) that this is called experiential avoidance. When you use experiential avoidance to manage your thoughts and feelings, you'll probably choose the most familiar or typical response to address a given situation, and you'll engage in that response in a rigid, inflexible way that doesn't help you effectively reach your goals. For example, had Ruth been caught up in experiential avoidance, she might have repeated—like a broken record—what she had done during the previous visit to the pizza restaurant. In the next section, we'll discuss how to use your emerging mindfulness skills to help build—or rebuild—your relationship with your child in a flexible, positive way.

Parenting Mindfully: Appreciating Your Child

When young children misbehave—for example, when they're argumentative and stubborn—their parents dislike being around them. Sound familiar? Because interactions are so unpleasant, you'll limit the time that you spend with your child and keep chats brief; you may feel like you're walking on eggshells. This was the case for Ruth and George in our example above.

On the other hand, when young children are inhibited or feel anxious about things, parents usually react differently. Think of your own responses. If you're prone to worry yourself, you may find it very difficult to tolerate your child's struggle with anxiety. Thus, you may behave in ways that are intrusive and controlling to better manage how your child feels. For example, if your child struggles in doing a difficult puzzle, you may do it for her so that you're protected from her—and your own—negative feelings. However, this has negative consequences; it can discourage independent learning and mastery of different situations. Nonanxious parents tend to be more flexible with this.

However, even when your child doesn't struggle with anxiety, certain developmental issues can create challenging situations (see chapter 2). As your child becomes more autonomous and tests limits, or transitions to school, you'll undoubtedly face stressful situations that you must negotiate. Similarly parenting is only one part of your life. You may have many different responsibilities and experience a variety of stressors—from work, finances, other relationships, or your own emotional difficulties. All of these situations can create contexts in which you may be absentminded, preoccupied, or only partially present in your relationships with your child. When such contexts present themselves, you may fall into knee-jerk parenting behaviors and narrowly negative expectations of your child.

When this happens, your relationship with your child may change. If you focus on negative behaviors, you may experience your child as a set of problems to be solved. Many parents go through periods like this, so you're not alone; these periods are often difficult to acknowledge, much less talk about. You may find yourself relying on control strategies (see chapter 4). Unfortunately these are often unworkable, as you've probably seen from previous exercises in this book. Emotion control strategies or experiential avoidance can lead to almost exclusive focus on and fusion with your thoughts and emotions. The result? You fail to see your child as a whole, complete, and amazing little being. For instance, you might be caught up in thinking about past events, or what your child might do wrong next, or how you will feel if he misbehaves again. You might simply be preoccupied with other things—such as work, social obligations, finances, or other relationships—and might not be fully present in moments with your child. Consider the following quote:

> *If we are not fully ourselves, truly in the present moment, we miss everything. When a child presents himself to you with his smile, if you are not really there—thinking about the future or the past, or preoccupied with other problems—then the child is not really there for you. The technique of being alive is to go back to yourself in order for the child to appear like a marvelous reality. Then you can see him smile and you can embrace him in your arms.*
>
> Thich Nhat Hanh

Seeing Your Child as a Whole Person

When you experience challenging situations in your life or with your child, you may find it very difficult to notice broader aspects of your experience. For example, you might notice your child misbehaving but not the color of his eyes, how he's looking at you, what happened to trigger his actions, or your own behavior in response to his. Cultivating mindfulness skills in the time you spend with your child is one way to begin to build—or rebuild—this lost awareness.

Present, Past, and Future

Our minds, and the language that we use to communicate what goes on in them, can bring the past and future right into this very moment. When we learn to mindfully (that is, nonjudgmentally) experience our past and our future in the present moment, we're able to see experiences as if they're really happening in the here and now and, all the while, be open to seeing things in a whole new way. Possibilities can open up when we get mindful exposure to our past and future in the present moment. For example, your child might be struggling in her kindergarten class, and yet you might imagine her on her college graduation day—and then work your hardest to make sure that she gets all the academic help she needs to make sure that day actually happens.

Now try the following guided meditation and see where it takes you. Read through the exercise once or twice so you don't have to refer back to the book during the meditation.

EXERCISE: Remember When?

Find a few minutes for quiet reflection. Sit in a comfortable chair and close your eyes.

Bring your mind back to your earliest memories of your child as a newborn. Bring yourself back into the skin of the person you were in that moment. Notice the small size and weight of your child, how he smelled, the delicate softness of his skin. Bring yourself back into that moment and notice how you felt—perhaps joyful, peaceful, or in awe of this completely new, amazing little being, and the terror of your new responsibility.

Notice that this small, vulnerable, incredibly strong little child, for whom the whole world would open up in limitless possibility, is the same person today as he was then. See if you can see his face now that he has grown. See if you can see traces of that newborn in his face now. He still carries now the same vulnerability and strength you felt then. See if you can make a space for that vulnerability and strength in a compassionate way as you come back to the present.

Skills for Building Your Relationship with Your Child

What was it like for you to participate in the previous meditation? What if you could gently hold that rich, full experience of your child in your awareness regardless of what your child is doing in the moment? Part of mindful awareness is noticing the continuity of your experience: when your child struggles and when you as a parent struggle, you're the same beings in your worst moments as you are in your best moments. One way to help hold that understanding in your awareness is to expect, with compassion, your child to do the next right thing. Very often parents expect the worst, especially in times of great stress. You don't have to believe this of your child—indeed, if you argue with your mind about whether she will or won't, you'll slip out of the moment into the hypothetical future. You can choose, however, to simply act with that awareness of your thoughts while holding this thought: *My child can do the next right thing.* If your mind wanders into the negative, such as unpleasant memories or worries about the future, simply acknowledge that and gently lead your mind back to the moment. We'll give you some ideas for holding this awareness of your thoughts as well as for "skillfully noticing" the many facets of your child in the exercise below.

Many parent training programs contain activities that aim to enhance parent–child relationships. We believe that such activities may be enhanced even more if parents learn to practice mindful awareness while doing them. One way to begin to gain a richer awareness of your child is to practice mindfulness during pleasant interactions with him. (In the next chapter, we'll talk more about how your mindfulness skills can be useful in difficult interactions with your child.)

EXERCISE: Simply Being with Your Child

This is an ongoing exercise or practice of mindfulness. Make some time daily—even ten to fifteen minutes—to spend time with your child. You may describe it to your child as "special time." If you have other children, choose a time when they're otherwise engaged or being watched by a partner, spouse, or friend. It's helpful if can you plan ahead and clear your schedule so you won't be interrupted or tempted to take care of other obligations or responsibilities. Determine the best time of day for you and your child (for example, after a nap or a meal but not during his favorite TV program or prime sibling or neighborhood playdate time).

During this time, allow your child to choose whatever activity he'd like to do. If your child is younger, perhaps two to four years old, it may be useful for you to give two or three choices of activities. Older children (beyond age five) are much more capable of independently choosing what they'd like to do from a broad variety of toys or games. After your child has made his choice, simply play with him. Follow your child's lead. Resist asking questions, giving directions, or making negative comments. Rather practice noticing everything that's going on in the situation—what your child is doing, his goals, what he says, how his face looks, how he seems to feel. Notice also how you feel— your thoughts, feelings, and emotions. As you notice different facets of your experience, practice putting them into words for your child like a sports commentator might. For example, if your child is playing with trucks in a sandbox, you might comment on what he's doing, something like this: "You're making the red truck go really fast! It's a fire truck, and now it's climbing the sand mountain and going to the town. I see some buildings and other cars there too. There must be a fire. Wow, that truck is in a hurry!" (Hembree-Kigin and McNeil 1995). Reflect and expand on what your child says. Comment on how your child might be feeling. For example, to build on the example above, you might say, "You must be happy to have such a fast fire truck!" Perhaps your child responds, "He wants to save the people in the burning house." You might respond, "He's going fast to save those people. He's a very brave fireman!" Most of all, listen, and take it all in.

There's a Buddhist saying that, paraphrased, is something like "Don't speak unless you can improve on the silence." Practice simply being present with your child. Don't try to change or solve anything, or help, or redirect. There is no need. Simply be. Appreciate the fullness of the moment. Over time, you may notice that the quality of your interactions may change. You're more able to see things as they are without immediate reaction—for example, when your child pours juice all over the counter and it doesn't anger you, and you might even find some humor in it. It's easier to have more fun with your child, and the time may begin to feel richer as you can mindfully see multiple aspects of your experience.

Mindfully Motivating Good Behavior

Previously we mentioned that practicing mindfulness does not necessarily mean stillness or not acting. Indeed, in our series of exercises, you practiced mindfulness in a variety of different contexts and across activities. Now you'll be able to practice your mindfulness skills in a very purposeful way—to motivate your child's good behavior. Try the exercise below to see how to do this.

EXERCISE: A Little Praise Can Go a Long Way

Even when your child is at her worst, she still does things that are good some of the time. Take a minute to think about a few behaviors that your child does that you would like her to do more frequently or consistently. For example, you might choose using manners, sharing, or helping around the house, depending on how old your child is. As you think about those behaviors, try to describe them so that any observer would be able to tell whether your child was doing them or not. For example, to be very clear about what you are looking for, you might write "sharing toys with his friends" rather than simply "sharing." List three such behaviors in your journal.

If you're like most parents, you probably spend more time on addressing misbehavior than positive behavior. After all, you probably expect your child to behave and see little need to reward her for what she *should* be doing anyway. Yet see what you think of these questions: Are you willing to work for free? When you've had employers, did you prefer to work for those who let you know when you'd done a good job or those that didn't seem to notice? In a similar vein, how do you know or how did you learn necessary skills at work? Children need much the same guidance. When behaviors are attended to and nurtured, they grow stronger and occur more frequently. This process is called *reinforcement* (see chapter 3). Behavior that goes unnoticed may weaken and disappear.

See if throughout the day you can mindfully notice your child engaging in the three behaviors you have listed above. Each time your child does one of these behaviors, do the following:

1. Say "Good job doing X" or "I really like how you did X!" Make sure you're very specific. Letting your child know exactly what it was that she did well helps her to understand how to do it in the future. For example, when your child puts her dishes in the sink, be sure to say, "Good job of putting away your dishes. Thank you." This is more effective than just saying "Good job" or "Thanks."

2. Be genuine—don't fake it. See if you can really stay in the moment with your child and look her in the eyes as you praise her.

3. If the desired behavior occurs with misbehavior, see if you can focus on the good behavior and respond to it, while being mindful of the misbehavior and not reacting to that. For example, if your child shares but initially resists and whines, you might ignore that initial reluctance and praise the sharing.

The technique described here is called *labeled praise*, and it will help you shape positive behavior in your child. At the beginning, try to praise your child every time she does a particular action, especially if it's not one she does very frequently. See if you notice any changes in the frequency, strength, or deliberation with which your child does these things that you're praising.

Mindfully Dealing with Behavior

It can be very difficult to maintain a mindful stance when you're in the middle of a difficult interaction with your child. Nonetheless, you can develop this ability if you practice mindfulness over time and across situations. As we've structured our exercises in this chapter, you started by practicing mindful awareness in simple situations like while you're breathing or sitting. Now try to gradually extend your practice into situations where you're doing things—walking, cooking, shopping, playing with your child, and eventually when you're dealing with your child's difficult behaviors.

Remember, mindfulness is a nonjudgmental, compassionate, accepting awareness of all facets of your—or your child's—experience without attempts to change it. In fact, the goal of mindfulness is to increase your psychological flexibility—that is, your awareness of and ability to choose among an array of possible actions in the service of your values.

Summary

In this chapter, we discussed the use of mindfulness skills. Mindfulness is broken down into a number of components, including the description of your experience, acting with awareness, acceptance of your experience, and non-reactivity. In ACT, self-as-context (that is, the observer you), defusion, and contact with the present moment are used to help foster mindfulness. Several exercises helped you practice your emerging mindfulness skills, which will develop further with time and practice. Finally, we offered you some opportunities to use your mindfulness skills to help build your relationship with your child and to motivate good behavior.

In the next chapter, we'll discuss the use of mindfulness in the context of willingness and committed action. We'll also illustrate how mindfulness allows you to more fully pursue your values. Finally, we'll advise you how to address your child's misbehavior.

CHAPTER 6

Doing What Works, Not What's Easy

Standing for Your Child

*There are only two mistakes one can make along the road to truth;
not going all the way, and not starting.*

Buddha

Do, or do not. There is no try.

Yoda

It's one thing to learn to use the skills presented in this book in a conceptual way, or to think about using them as you are reading. It's entirely another to put them into active, effective practice. You may have many other things to do, and you feel you don't have enough hours in the day to really practice what you learn. Or you may argue with your mind about what's possible for you and your child or whether this stuff is worth the work. Maybe while doing the exercises in chapter 5, you noticed that arguing with your mind stopped your attempts to practice your skills before you really started. When these or other experiences threaten to get you off course, remember the values you want to live out in your relationship with your child. And then just notice and welcome your thoughts and worries about putting what you read into practice. Let them join you as you read this chapter. Let them come or go as they please, and choose to parent according to your values, no matter what you think or feel.

Practicing new skills is hard for all parents, and it's especially difficult in times of stress or transition. However, parenting skills—no matter what approach you learn, how motivating it is, or how well you study—are irrelevant if you don't actively use them. So the choice set before you is, as Yoda says, to "do, or do not." The choice you make is entirely up to you; however, you might feel like you don't have a choice when you are overwhelmed about your parenting. When you find yourself feeling like your behavior "just happens" or that you "have to" parent in a specific way, both your values and your commitment to following your values fade. Thus, in this chapter, you'll learn about seeing choices and making them in ways that are consistent with your values. We'll address the concepts of "willingness" and "committed action" and teach you how to bring them to bear in your challenging interactions with your child. In working through these concepts, we'll teach you some effective parenting strategies that you can use to address your child's misbehaviors.

Willingness: Having What You've Got

Willingness is like giving yourself permission to think what you think and feel what you feel without trying to change or control it—no matter how good or bad it seems. It also refers to letting go of fighting the circumstances in your life that you can't change. Willingness is usually done in the service of some important possibility. For example, it might be important for you to allow yourself to feel guilty so that you don't always give in to your child's tantrums. If you are willing, you might end up teaching your child some more effective behavior rather than just doing something to make your own feelings of guilt go away.

So, more specifically, what ACT means by willingness as it relates to parenting is just having whatever thoughts and feelings you might experience about using a particular parenting strategy without fighting them. This is particularly important if you experience painful thoughts and feelings and are still committed to consistently living the values you hold for yourself and your child. To illustrate what we mean by willingness, please complete the following exercise. Write your answers in your parenting journal. And remember that your mind can bring the past and future into this moment, and, if you are mindful, you may learn something new.

EXERCISE: Noticing Willingness in Challenging Situations

1. Take a moment to think of a recent challenging situation with your child.

2. Close your eyes and get present to that situation. See if you can notice all aspects of it as if you're experiencing it once again: Where are you? Whom are you with? What's going on around you? What's your child doing? What are you thinking and feeling?

3. Give yourself permission to have all of those experiences without fighting against them or changing them in any way. Consider that there may be something important in those experiences for you and for your child.

How did this exercise feel to you? Becoming present to a difficult situation with your child may not be very pleasant for you, so we want to acknowledge your courage in doing this. Though you may not know it, by doing this exercise you've taken important steps toward understanding this difficult situation in a broader and potentially more helpful way. We mentioned this briefly in chapter 5 when we talked about the quality of mindful interactions with your child, and we'll come back to this mindful approach to this difficult problem later in this chapter.

As we mentioned earlier, there will be contexts—times, places, circumstances—when coping with your child's behavior is more or less difficult for you, or when you're more or less willing to deal with it. For instance, you may find it harder to address a misbehavior when you're in public than in private. Or, if you feel less sure of yourself or your skills, you may be less willing to deal with inappropriate behavior. You may also feel more or less willing depending on whom you are with or how busy you are with other areas of your life, such as your relationship with your partner, work, or finances. Because it's important for you to recognize how contexts influence your parenting behavior, take a few minutes to complete the short exercise below.

EXERCISE: Contexts That Affect My Willingness

Identify five contexts or situations in which you feel more or less willing to address your child's actions. Place them in order from least to most difficult, with least difficult being 1 and most difficult being 5. Write this list in your parenting journal.

Willingness Is a Choice, Not a Feeling

In thinking through the exercise above and making a hierarchy of situations in which you felt more or less willing to address your child's actions, you may have come into contact with willingness as a feeling. Sometimes being willing feels easy—as, for example, having willingness to feel proud of your child after she accomplishes something big. At other times, willingness feels very hard to achieve. For example, being embarrassed in a large crowd of people who watch your child whining may not feel like something you are willing, or even able, to do. In other words, you may have felt more or less motivated to address your child's behavior or even to simply withstand that behavior across situations, settings, or people. However, although willingness certainly includes what you're feeling, it's not *simply* a feeling. You may feel willing or unwilling. Either one is just fine—and yet neither has much bearing on what you *choose* to do. In other words, you could feel willing and not act, or you could feel unwilling and choose to act anyway. It's sort of like driving with a really noisy backseat driver who yells out directions or critiques your driving. If you're driving, you can go in whatever direction you want to go, regardless of that backseat driver. After all, it's your car, isn't it?

This "backseat driver," of course, is simply your mind doing what it does best: trying to protect you from harm. However, your mind—if it's like the minds of most other humans—may prefer to play it safe and try to protect you from losses rather than to play for a big win. A "big win" might be long-term improvements in your relationship with your child or in your child's behavior. A "loss" might be feeling embarrassed or experiencing your child's discomfort in the short run. When you choose to play for protection from losses rather than for big wins, you may actually experience losses that are bigger than what you consider acceptable.

How might this work with your child? Let's say you have to give your child a time-out in order to discourage a misbehavior, but you know that if you do so, he'll throw a tantrum. That tantrum will embarrass you. As you think about your choices—to give the time-out or not—your mind kicks in and tells you that other parents will laugh, that you'll feel ashamed, that if your child throws a fit, it means you're a terrible parent, and so on. Your mind may give you a list of reasons why you shouldn't go through with the time-out, as a way to protect you from these imagined—or perhaps very real—experiences. Yet what is lost is your effective management of your child's behavior. In addition, by not giving the time-out, you may contribute to the worsening of that behavior. Perhaps you choose to give the time-out, as it is part of your committed action toward your values. We will come back to committed action later in the chapter. For now, just consider this: When you value something, like teaching your child to follow important rules or to communicate her desires in an appropriate way, there are certain behaviors that go along with that. You choose to be committed to those actions and then do them even when doing them is hard. Thus, we sometimes speak of willingness as action. Try the following guided meditation to get a sense of willingness as action.

EXERCISE: Driving to School

Read through the entire exercise once or twice, and then, when you're ready, begin.

Get into a comfortable position. Close your eyes, or focus on a spot on the wall or floor. Take a few deep breaths. Notice how your breath feels going in and out, how your chest and abdomen rise and fall with your breath.

Let your attention shift now and think about driving your child to school. Imagine that your child has to be at school by 7:45 a.m. and that she has no other way to get there. See if you can picture the two of you in the car together. Imagine all of the steps of the morning routine that got you to the car—getting out of bed, waking her up, having breakfast, making sure that she turns off the TV and gets dressed—whatever your normal process is. Gently notice whatever thoughts and feelings you're having about that process.

Now imagine that you went to bed at 9 p.m. the night before; you slept well and easily woke up on your own at 6:00 a.m. You slowly drank a couple of cups of coffee and read the paper or watched some entertaining TV show. You're in a great mood. Notice how you feel about the drive to school.

Shift your focus to a different kind of day. Imagine that you were up all night tossing and turning, that you have a lot of work to get done, and that you have an appointment with your child's teacher later. Notice how you feel about the drive now.

Still considering that day when you're tired because you didn't sleep well, let your attention expand out, to imagine what it means for your child to get an education. Recognize for a moment that this requires getting her to school on time. Now picture yourself getting up, going through the morning routine, being in the car with her. Notice what thoughts, feelings, bodily sensations, or memories show up when you place your attention on these events. See if you can take them along with you on the drive. Allow them to be passengers because your child's education matters to you.

Finally, notice that you can get into the car and drive to school no matter what you're thinking or feeling about doing it. Sometimes it'll feel easier than other times. Remember, willingness isn't just a feeling. It's a choice.

Willingness often involves a course of action that's consistent with your values, independent of your thoughts and feelings. Your chosen actions should take you in the direction of the things you value, not simply *appear* to be doing so. The following story illustrates what this might look like in a fairly common parenting situation.

✤ Learning to Play: Looking Helpful vs. Being Helpful

Joyce's daughter, Chelsea, is six years old and in first grade at a new school. Chelsea expresses some worries to her mother, saying that she doesn't know how to join games with the other kids on the playground. She has a few friends, but not many. Joyce speaks to a psychologist about Chelsea's worries, and the clinician recommends that Chelsea be given more opportunity to learn developmentally appropriate social skills—such as starting conversations, asking politely to join a game, and refusing politely when she chooses not to participate. The overall goal of this is for her to make friends. Joyce identifies her own value as a parent as supporting Chelsea in developing meaningful, balanced friendships.

Now at pickup time after school, Joyce lingers to provide Chelsea with more opportunities to watch and participate in social play with the other children. However, each time she sees her daughter struggle, hang back from games, or withdraw in response to some perceived slight, Joyce steps in and tries to control the situation. She pulls her daughter out of the situations and talks with her, or she tries to interject herself into the children's conversation so that she might manage it. This has become such a pattern that Chelsea's teacher has become annoyed with Joyce's behavior, and she takes a few moments to express her concerns to Joyce. The teacher points out that it disrupts the children's play and actually seems to interfere with the development of Chelsea's emerging social repertoire because it prevents her from trying things on her own. The teacher also feels that it gives Chelsea the idea that she isn't capable of being comfortable and competent socially without her mother's help. Joyce becomes angry and takes an adversarial stance with the teacher. She talks about her dissatisfaction with the other parents. After this, Joyce receives several polite refusals from other parents when she attempts to arrange out-of-school playdates between their children and Chelsea, who is becoming more and more lonely and nervous on the playground.

Looking Willing vs. Being Willing

Joyce attempted to help her daughter. Although Joyce's stated value was to help Chelsea develop meaningful friendships, her choice of actions may have actually prevented that from happening. You might say that her parenting tactics were more about protecting her daughter from discomfort—or even protecting herself from experiencing her own discomfort while watching her daughter struggle—than supporting the development of Chelsea's social skills. It might have looked like Joyce was willing to have her experiences—and Chelsea's as well—because she was trying to create a lot of opportunities for growth. However, her willingness was quite conditional: she was only willing to provide those opportunities when she felt like things were going well. Really being willing would have resulted in her continued support of Chelsea's social skill development, no matter how each of them felt. What might have been more useful to her daughter would have been to trust that Chelsea was capable of figuring out the situation on her own and that she didn't need protection from her own feelings. Ironically, if her mom stood back and didn't intercede, that might have *looked* like, or even *felt,* to Joyce that she was being unhelpful. Here we see a clear example of the difference between *looking* helpful and *being* helpful in a values-consistent way. The outcome of "looking helpful" was, despite Joyce's good intentions, a situation that became worse than it was before. And that was inconsistent with Joyce's values.

As a parent, you'll have many opportunities to choose between looking willing and truly being willing to pursue your values. And in order to detect whether your chosen course of action is values-consistent or not, you need to discriminate between looking willing and being willing. In order to determine whether you're looking willing or being willing, you should go back to the functional analysis skills that you learned in chapter 4. This is a time that your mind will be very useful to you.

Think back to your Contexts that Affect my Willingness list from the exercise earlier in this chapter. You listed some situations in which willingness to experience your thoughts and feelings would be very hard. Pick a situation that was on your list at number 3, 4, or 5. Take a moment now to think of willingness as action for the situation that you chose. You will need to first identify a value related to that situation. Then, in your parenting journal, write down three committed actions related to moving toward that value. Next, consider a time that you have done one of those actions. Allow yourself to get present to that and then write down what happened just before and after you performed the action. What did it do for you and for your child? Looking at the antecedents and consequences will help you figure out the function of your action. If it resulted in you looking good to others, or if you did it to avoid feeling bad, chances are you only did that behavior to *look* willing. If it resulted in your feeling like you had done something important for you and your child, you were probably *being* willing. Sometimes you'll notice that being willing still looks or feels bad, so you can't really determine willingness based on how you feel or what the outcome is. Therefore, willingness to engage in values-consistent action does not mean

- that you will not make mistakes;

- that you have failed if you do make mistakes; or

- that you must be sure about what to do in order to act.

Notice that vitality and importance does not make willingness easy—nor does being willing automatically result in values-consistent behavior.

Willingness Is Often All-or-Nothing

What did the functional analysis reveal about your parenting strategies? Chances are you learned that you parent inconsistently—that is, you do different things in different situations for different reasons. Perhaps you feel that being willing to parent consistently is something you can accomplish gradually, over time, much like the practice of mindful awareness. Although you've already identified situations in which you feel more or less willing, it's important to understand that willingness is often an "all-or-nothing" endeavor. Remember the Zen saying "Leap and the net will appear" that was introduced in chapter 3? Willingness is a choice to leap—unconditionally, no matter what. There's no such thing as being partly willing (Hayes, Strosahl, and Wilson 1999). This is especially true in parenting, where behaving consistently in a variety of situations is extremely important, as we'll see in the story below.

✤ *I Want It NOW!*

Zach is working with his four-year-old son Taylor, who tends to demand things. In the past, Taylor rarely asked for things politely. Instead he said things like "I want this" or "Get me a snack NOW." He did this with his father, his teacher, and other children. His preschool teacher told Zach that Taylor's behavior was disrupting his play with the other children and that Taylor was more frequently playing by himself. So now when Zach is at home, he makes sure before he gives Taylor what he wants that Taylor says "please" and uses a polite tone of voice. If Taylor can't have what he wants, Zach sticks to his guns, no matter what. Sometimes Taylor throws huge tantrums, falls down on the floor, throws his toys, or screams at Zach. It's really hard for Zach, but he doesn't give in.

One day Zach takes Taylor to a party with some of his coworkers and their children. Even his boss's family is there. The event is going well until Taylor refuses to eat a meal and insists on having ice cream instead. "NO! I don't want a burger. ICE CREAM! Daddy, I want it!" Zach tries to say no and to quietly steer Taylor away from the cooler full of ice cream, but Taylor plants his feet and yells louder.

People stare and chuckle nervously. "Taylor, please cut it out," *Zach hisses.* "NO, BUT I WANT ICE CREAM NOW!" *Zach sees his boss tilt his head in their direction. His mind starts racing: What will my boss think? Taylor's making me look so bad! Zach feels a flare of anger and desperation. This was so predictable—why won't Taylor just stop it?* "Okay," *Zach says,* "but just this once ... if you be quiet!" *And he hands Taylor an ice cream.*

Willingness Is Critical to Consistent Parenting

This type of situation is probably a typical one for you and most parents. For Zach, his willingness to stick to set limits with Taylor was conditional—in other words, he was willing only when it wasn't too hard. When things got really tough—as they do for all parents—Zach bailed out on his parenting strategy of holding the line. Rainer Maria Rilke, the German poet, once wrote "There are no classes in life for beginners; right away, you are always asked to do what is most difficult." Unfortunately this is particularly true for parents, and it speaks to the all-or-nothing quality of willingness. In the case of Zach, his conditional, intermittent use of holding the line and giving in will contribute to Taylor's misbehavior becoming more persistent and intense. This is because the consequence of Taylor's demanding behavior was that he got what he wanted. Thus, the next time Zach says no to something his son demands, Taylor will throw a tantrum and demand again, because it worked the first time. Zach's inconsistent parenting also makes it hard for Taylor to learn the rules. So, as a parent, being conditionally willing can intensify your child's unwanted behaviors. We'll come back to the importance of consistent parenting later in this chapter. Please work through the exercise below to explore your own use of parenting strategies where you may be only conditionally willing.

EXERCISE: The Consequences of Conditional Willingness

Look at the list you made earlier of contexts that affect your willingness. One at a time, consider each context on the list. Focus on how you typically respond in the least and most difficult situations. Note the similarities and differences of your responses in each situation.

Spend a few moments considering the direction in which those behaviors take you. Do they move you toward or away from your valued course? Take a few moments to record your responses—and your thoughts and feelings about them—in your parenting journal.

Steve Hayes and colleagues (1999) write about willingness as "the primary condition for committed action." You can't make a meaningful commitment to follow through on something without the essential ingredient of willingness. As you've seen, willingness is also crucial to effective, consistent parenting across a variety of contexts. In the next section, we'll discuss what's meant by commitment or committed action, and you'll discover what's involved in making a commitment to stand for your child no matter what.

Committed Action: Living by Your Values

Willingness means choosing to make a commitment in the service of your values. When you value something, like teaching your child an appropriate way to communicate her desires, there are certain behaviors that go along with that. You choose to do those actions even when doing them is hard. *Committed action*, therefore, is doing the things that allow you to reach value-consistent goals and move in the direction of what you care about. Commitment is unconditional: it means doing the actions that bring you toward what you care about most for you and for your child when you don't know how it will turn out and even when the outcome has been negative when you did the action in the past. For example, you can be committed to taking your child to school every day even though he is failing and getting in trouble. However, once you choose to make a commitment, you'll inevitably confront experiences you'd rather avoid. Perhaps this happened as you completed the exercises presented earlier. Discomfort like the discomfort you felt when working through the exercises has also been evident in the stories we've presented.

It's very important to parent consistently—in ways that truly support your child and what you want for him and that enhance your relationship with him. For example, you may hold the value of helping your child to have loving friendships and to be a good friend. You know that there are a number of smaller, more concrete behavioral goals that arise on the way to this valued direction. You may, for example, plan playdates, spend time in your child's classroom observing your child at play, and support your child's ability to negotiate arguments with friends. Or you may give negative consequences, like time-out or taking away a privilege for bullying or meanness. Some of these smaller goals may have costs for you: your time, the anxiety of seeing your child be rejected or left out, the embarrassment of seeing your child show unkindness to other children, or perhaps feelings of insecurity or discomfort when you speak with other parents on behalf of your child; your willingness will be challenged.

Barriers to Committed Action

Four factors affect your commitment to pursue your values—fusion, evaluation, avoidance, and reason-giving. Each of these factors can feel like a barrier to your valued course. For example, fusion with the thought *I am a bad parent* may result in your ignoring positive interactions with your child. Likewise, reason-giving—like *I didn't drive her to school because she should have gotten up earlier to take the bus*—may serve as a way for you to justify not taking your child to school (Hayes, Strosahl, and Wilson 1999). A good way to remember these factors is to think of the mnemonic FEAR, presented below.

■ **F**usion with your thoughts

■ **E**valuation of yourself or your experiences

■ **A**voidance of experiences

■ **R**eason-giving for your behavior

We've touched on these issues before, but let's take another look at them as barriers to committed action.

Fusion

Fusion, or having an attachment to your thoughts as real or literal, may be more pronounced when you experience great stress. For example, if you struggle with emotional issues, substance use, work-related difficulties, or relationship issues, parenting may feel more burdensome. You may be fused with the idea that parenting is just one more area of your life that takes a great deal of effort. In this case, you may find it especially difficult to add yet another commitment to a list that's potentially long and overwhelming already.

When you engage in committed action, you may find fusion rearing its ugly head in thoughts like these: *This parenting stuff is too hard, My child is not fixable, I messed up again, I don't know why I even try, I'm a horrible parent, Can I can get it right next time?* Defusing from these thoughts, perhaps by imagining them as leaves on a stream or as passing clouds, will help you to move forward.

Evaluation

Your mind can and will evaluate your committed actions in many different ways. You may, for example, value education for your child. So you might say, "I will get my child to school on time every day, no matter how I feel." Then your mind begins to evaluate and say things like EVERY day? That doesn't seem very reasonable. This type of evaluative thinking is self-defeating. When you find yourself stuck on self-defeating thoughts, take a deep breath, thank your mind for watching out for you, and consider what you hope for in that moment.

Evaluation can show up in other ways too. You choose to avoid making commitments in the area of parenting—either for yourself or for your child—because you're afraid that you can't keep them. Or you feel that values in other areas of your life compete with your parenting values. Notice, however, that each of these is an evaluation of your choice to pursue your values. In the former, you're evaluating yourself: can you stay on course or will you fail? In the latter, you're evaluating your choice of what to pursue. In either of these situations, choosing to engage in valued action may feel oppressive or at odds with things you want to do in other areas of your life. You may feel very confused. Just notice that, and know that confusion indicates that something matters to you.

Someone once said, "There are no bad decisions—only those we have to live with." You may notice your mind beating you up for choosing one course or the other; sometimes this interferes with committed action. Let's say you value your relationship with your child and you also choose to work at home during the evenings—to catch up on work that you didn't finish at the office or to get ahead for the next day. When you do this, you think, I'm not being a good parent; I'm not spending enough time with my child. You may feel bad about that, so you just work later at the office. And then you're likely to be upset by that, so you work even more hours so that you don't have to think about how you haven't kept up your commitment to your child. This is experiential avoidance. Your mind likely has something to say about that too! Give those evaluative thoughts a nod, and take them with you. When you choose to follow a course in a single area of your life, you're still making a choice: to follow the course—or follow a value—or not.

Avoidance

Experiential avoidance (see chapter 4) often prevents you from taking committed action. One way to detect experiential avoidance is to ask yourself the question "What am I working for?" If you're working to get rid of feeling bad as opposed to moving toward your values, then you probably aren't really doing committed action. In addition, pursuing valued action is *always* a choice. Most of the time, being consistent with your values is accompanied by a sense of importance and vitality. Sometimes when you engage in valued actions, however, the behavior may occur with the thought that "I must" or the feeling that doing so is oppressive or overwhelming. Your mind is trying to tell you to avoid. Notice those experiences and acknowledge that they, too, travel with you on your journey. Just like other chatter from your mind, these too are simply words—not real, and neither good nor bad. They may seem compelling, but they have little to do with your capacity to choose or to act.

Reason-Giving

Your mind is an expert in providing reasons for choosing or not choosing. After all, your mind's job is to be logical. It may tell you not to do something because you'll get hurt or because it hasn't worked in the past. Or it may tell you to do something because that's what smart people would do. Reasons, as we mentioned before, can serve as justification for doing something that isn't really values-consistent. For example, after making a valued choice to use time-out, if it does not go smoothly, you might say, "Time-out doesn't work for my child. He's too hyper. I should just spank him."

Following your values with integrity has little to do with logic: here's a case in which it's more helpful to consult your heart. When you repeatedly make the choice *to avoid* engaging in committed, valued action—such as giving your child a spanking instead of giving a time-out—you'll likely feel stuck or mired down. Your mind may tell you that this feeling stuck and your reluctance to get back on your valued course are things that simply "happened" to you—our minds are pretty good at tricking us into getting hooked on ideas like this. The idea that you had no role in choosing your behavior is a good story—it's a reason that your mind presents to choose pursuit of values or not. Nonetheless, being stuck, too, is a choice. You may think that you're "trying." For example, if you plan on using time-out, practice it with your child, and otherwise prepare for it, but if you then spank her in the heat of the moment for her negative behavior, you might say to yourself, *At least I tried—it just won't work.* Thank your mind for that evaluation; certainly, on the face of it, "trying" seems like a good reason *not* to honor a commitment to follow your values. Remember that this too is a choice: do, or do not. Every time you choose not to act or to act in a way that is inconsistent with your values, remember that you *are* choosing—also remember that you have another choice: you can think about the behaviors that are consistent with your values and commit to doing them. To get a better sense of what's meant by committed action, try the guided meditation below.

EXERCISE: Whatever It Takes: Unconditional Commitment

Imagine that your child is walking into a busy intersection. Cars and trucks whiz by, and your child isn't paying attention. She steps off the curb. You yell out to her, but the traffic is so loud that she can't hear you.

Take a moment to consider what you're thinking and feeling. Write down in your journal what you would do in a situation like this.

Chances are that, in that moment, you'd do whatever you needed to do to keep her safe, including rushing out into traffic yourself. You probably wouldn't think about all the times you taught her to look both ways and wait until traffic was clear, nor would you think about your own safety. And there's probably no one who could have logically, rationally talked you out of rushing into the street. You would likely willingly place yourself in danger in the service of protecting your child. This type of act—to move toward a purpose despite any obstacles, including those that might be unpleasant or risky—is what is meant by commitment.

Parenting Consistently

As mentioned early in this chapter, putting willingness and committed action into practice is easier said than done. As a parent of a young child, however, you'll face many situations in which using particular strategies *consistently*, especially when it's very hard to do so, is critical to success. Similarly a number of parenting strategies work *only* if consistently applied: using them inconsistently may actually worsen your child's behavior. Thus, when learning such strategies—especially for use in challenging situations—your willingness and commitment to valued actions are essential. One helpful strategy is called "planned ignoring." Let's take a look at planned ignoring now—what it is and how you can use it with your child.

Parenting Strategy: Planned Ignoring

One value that many parents may hold is helping their children live a meaningful life. This includes teaching their children to behave well. As a parent, you can accomplish this by shaping and nurturing appropriate behaviors as well as reducing or stopping inappropriate behaviors. The technique of mindfully motivating behavior through paying attention to it (for example, praising it) is one way to support your child's good behavior. The strategy of *planned ignoring*, in which you observe your child's behavior without reaction, helps to reduce or eliminate behaviors that you find unacceptable.

Very often your child engages in behaviors that are "annoying" because they get your attention or the attention of others. When these annoying behaviors "work" for your child, he tends to continue doing them. Even if his behaviors result in your scolding or redirecting him, they function (see chapter 4) in the way they were intended: to get one-on-one attention from you.

Thus, the best way to address these behaviors that your child does to get your attention is to ignore them—simply observe the behavior without reacting to it. If you're doing something else when your child performs an attention-seeking behavior, continue whatever you're doing—as long as it doesn't include an attempt to alter or change your child's irritating behavior in any way. Planned ignoring *does not* mean

- redirecting or scolding your child;

- making eye contact or giving her meaningful looks;

- retaliating for the annoying behavior in any way;

- negotiating with your child;

- reasoning with your child;

- commenting on the annoying behavior or commenting that you are ignoring him;

- removing your love or affection from your child;

- showing anger or irritation at your child;

- explaining to your child why she shouldn't do a particular behavior;

- asking your child *why* he did what he did; or

- punishing your child for the behavior later.

The metaphor of a faucet can help you understand how planned ignoring works: When your child engages in an annoying behavior, *immediately* turn off your attention the way you would a faucet. Be very clear and obvious in how you do this. Conversely, when your child stops the misbehavior, turn your attention back on. Heap her with praise. For example, when your child is yelling, turn your body away from him and do not say a word—turn off your attention. As soon as he gets quiet or lowers his voice to an appropriate volume, turn toward him, make good eye contact, and say, "I like the way that you used your inside voice" or something like that—turn your attention back on.

When you use the planned ignoring strategy, it's highly likely that your child will initially up the ante. In other words, he'll do the behavior you don't like—and he'll do it longer, harder, more frequently, or more intensely. During this phase, use your mindfulness skills: describing, acting with awareness, and not judging or reacting. You can hear your child screaming, for example, notice the screaming, and continue to ignore his behavior. Being willing to feel discomfort and maintain your commitment is critical. Practice experiencing your child's attention-seeking behavior as well as your own thoughts, emotions, and expectations, and the meanings you attribute to the behavior. Appreciate all of your reactions, and let them come or go at their own speed. Do this consistently each time your child acts out. Over time, if you apply planned ignoring consistently, you'll notice that your child will reduce or stop completely his attention-seeking behavior.

On Making Mistakes—and the Importance of Forgiveness

As you learn to use parenting strategies like planned ignoring as well as others that we'll present in this book, you'll make mistakes. You'll get hooked by your mind and find yourself behaving inconsistently with your values. It happens to all of us. When you notice that you've strayed from your course, simply acknowledge that and steer back toward your horizon, the values to which you're committed. Keep in mind that your course may not always be straight. You might need to navigate around a storm or some treacherous shoals. However, when you've deviated from your course, remember your commitment to your values and turn back in your chosen direction.

Sometimes your mind's chatter can divert you from renewing your commitment to your parenting values. Sometimes your mind leaves you feeling like a failure. Try this exercise as a way to help you with those feelings.

EXERCISE: Forgiving a Friend, Forgiving Yourself

1. Think of a time when you really felt like a failure as a parent or a time when you really messed up with your child. Remember everything that you can about that experience—where you were, what your child was doing, how you were feeling. See if you can remember any other details— the sounds and the smells, or any other memories linked to this one. Really put yourself back into that situation as if you're experiencing it again right now. Gently notice what's present in your mind and in your heart. Sit with the experience for a few moments.

2. Now imagine that your best friend is describing this experience to you as if it's happening to her. Notice what you feel for her. What do you want to do? What would you tell her?

3. Once again imagine yourself back in that same situation. Observe yourself as if you're watching a movie of your life. Pause, rewind, or fast-forward as necessary to allow yourself to experience the events fully. Look at your face, how you hold your body, and where you are in relation to your child. What are you thinking and feeling? What are you saying and doing?

4. What would you tell that parent in that moment, the you who has just made a parenting mistake, knowing now in this moment how that feels? Imagine having a conversation with yourself, much like the one you had with your friend. Allow yourself to feel for yourself that same compassion and forgiveness.

5. Your mind is good at telling you what to do—what you need to be safe, to protect yourself from looking foolish, to look right. But your mind also makes it difficult for you to forgive, especially to forgive yourself and those closest to your heart. Take a few moments to notice if it was easy or hard to forgive your friend for making a parenting mistake. And what about forgiving yourself? How was that—easy or hard? Did you experience some sense of relief when you forgave yourself? What about warmth or sensitivity? Now take a moment to think about how much compassion and

forgiveness would mean to your child when he messes up. Write down any reactions or thoughts that you have about that in your journal. What would it be like—for you and for your child—if he really knew that you loved and supported him unconditionally?

Making Your Own Commitment

You may not always like your child's behavior, but letting her know that—no matter what she does—you are there for her is an incredibly powerful way of parenting. Now, keeping that in mind, we'd like you to make a commitment to and for your child. Just the fact that you're working through this book shows your commitment to being a better parent. It shows that you care greatly about your child. In asking you to make a commitment for your child, we're asking you to take a big step toward unconditional support of her being. What we mean by that is choosing actions that would move you toward what you want for your child—and sticking to the choice no matter what. To do this, it's not necessary to know what to do or how to do it—in other words, you don't need to know now what's specifically involved in making such a commitment. You simply need to know what it is that you care most about in parenting your child. Sometimes we call this "standing for your child" because you can imagine a parent being firmly grounded to a valued course, with winds blowing to and fro, and with clouds all around, not budging.

EXERCISE: Standing for Your Child—in a Bigger, Bolder Way

1. Now is the time to play for big stakes. Think of your greatest hopes and dreams for your child. Think of your most extraordinary wishes for your relationship with him. Consider what you would have to do to achieve those greatest hopes and wishes, and predict the positive consequences for following through.

2. Specifically, what goals would you need to achieve to move your child and your relationship with him toward your values? Goals should be concrete and measurable. These may be specific behaviors to work on with respect to your parenting, or they may be aspects of your child's behavior that you would like to help improve. Write down a few behavioral goals that you will carry with you through the next few chapters so that you may track your success. You will likely be more successful if these goals are

small ones. Remember, these are commitments to your child and your relationship with him.

3. Notice and set aside your mind's evaluations of what is really possible or what you might lose. Notice your emotions and set them aside, or you may choose to allow your thoughts and feelings to travel the course with you.

4. If you could choose a life for your child—any life, unrestrained—what would that look like now and in the future? What would your child have in his life? Where would he be, whom would he be with, and what would he be doing? How would you support your child in discovering his talents, following his dreams, celebrating his successes, and coping with his disappointments? And what would you like your role to be in that life? What do you need to do to fulfill this role—what is your commitment?

5. Consider what you are willing to do to help these values come to be. Would anything stand in your way?

6. In identifying your parenting values and choosing your goals, many thoughts and emotions may flood your mind. The goal you have chosen may be one you have tried in the past, and you may have some anger or resentment that arises toward yourself, your partner, or your child. You may have blame for yourself or significant others in your child's life—your partner, your child's caregivers or teachers, the parents of your child's friends. Can you compassionately offer forgiveness to yourself and/or your child in making your commitment to follow your valued course? Write about this in your parenting journal.

7. It's often helpful to enlist the help of others in pursuit of a valued goal. Are there people in your life to whom you may express the commitments you thought of in the exercise and to whom you may go for help, support, or a break when things get difficult? Are you willing to ask for help when you need it? Write about your willingness to build a team of support for your commitments, consider with whom you might discuss this, and plan how you might start a conversation around your goal.

If you choose to act based on the commitments you came up with, you're ready to continue on to the remaining chapters on parenting strategies. Standing for your child will not always be easy—in fact, there will be many times when it will be very, very hard. And it will also be vitalizing and rewarding—and scary—all at the same time. If you choose not to accept any aspects of this commitment, honor that. Check out your experience and see if your mind is at work—notice and appreciate it in its process. Next, revisit your parenting values and the committed actions that go along with them with an open heart: because you have one life and one chance to make a difference for your child, would this be the value you would choose? If it is, when you're ready, move forward through the remainder of the book.

Summary

In this chapter, we discussed the concepts of willingness and committed action. Willingness is a critical ingredient in helping you to pursue your parenting values with integrity. You completed a number of experiential exercises to help you develop a sense of what is meant by willingness. Commitment is an unconditional choice to stand for your values, even when things are at their most difficult. We began to discuss parenting strategies—in particular, planned ignoring—in which your willingness and committed action can be brought to bear. Finally, we gave you an opportunity to make a meaningful commitment to advocate for your child. That commitment will help you as you continue through our book and learn to effectively use parenting strategies to support your parenting values.

CHAPTER 7

Building Your Relationship and Encouraging Good Behavior

We have more possibilities available in each moment than we realize.

Thich Nhat Hanh

In earlier chapters, we discussed times when it feels like it's hard to appreciate your child or even to be with him. This may be especially true when you're feeling vulnerable, tired, or stressed—or when your child's behavior seems really challenging. Imagine what it would be like if you enjoyed each other and experienced pleasure in simply being together. Each moment with your child is an opportunity to build your relationship and to encourage good behavior, even during the most difficult situations. In this chapter, we'll discuss how to build or rebuild your relationship with your child and how to see and encourage the best in him. This is an essential base for developing sensitive, responsive parenting strategies.

What Is a Good Relationship?

Take a moment to think about the relationships in your life that are most important to you—those in which you feel closest to someone else. What is it about those relationships that you most value? Take a few moments and jot down your thoughts about this in your parenting journal.

If you're like many parents, one of the valued characteristics you listed may have been "feeling heard." When we're very lucky, we find ourselves in relationships in which people "get" us—they have a solid understanding of our wants, desires, and dreams. They communicate that understanding in how they behave around us—by calling our attention to things we care about or being thoughtful without being asked and without expecting anything in return. Because these things are important to you, you won't be surprised that these same attributes are probably what your child most values and trusts about her relationship with you.

Taking time to nurture a relationship like this with your child is important. After all, you're the "base" from which your child ventures out into the world. You ensure his safety and offer a lens through which he will view other important relationships throughout his life. You show your young child how to be in the world by the way you relate to and behave with him. And that is an enormous responsibility—as well as an exquisite gift.

In order for your child to feel heard, it's important to be "attuned" to your child. *Attunement* means having a rich, detailed understanding of your child. As you become more attuned to your child, you'll be able to empathize with her thoughts and feelings, respond to her wishes, and facilitate her goals. You will also be able to better predict what your child will do next and to take in new information about your child as she grows—even when it might be inconsistent with your past experience of her. In short, attunement means openness to your child, and this capacity will help you to respond in a sensitive, caring way to her needs. Mindful awareness is an extremely helpful way to become fully present to your child and to enhance your attunement to her.

Find some time—about fifteen minutes—for the exercise below, in which you'll explore some ideas for nurturing your relationship with your child.

EXERCISE: Building an Attuned Relationship with Your Child

1. Think of a time when your child was learning something brand-new— maybe taking her first steps, or writing his own name or tying his shoes for the first time, or even taking her first breath. Write the time you're thinking of in your parenting journal.

2. Now close your eyes and take five to ten minutes to consider what that experience was like for each of you at that time. Really put yourself back in that space. Imagine it now in as much detail as possible: Where are you? What is that place like? Where is your child? What are you thinking, feeling, and experiencing as bodily sensations? What does your face look like? What does your child's face look like? Consider what he's wondering about and feeling. Is there vitality in that moment? Does it feel life-giving for your child, for you? Write your reactions to these questions in your journal.

3. Imagine now that your child makes a mistake—falls down, misspells, or otherwise struggles with carrying out this new skill successfully. Really feel that experience in this moment. What is it like for you? How do you think your child experiences this moment? How would you hope to respond in this situation? Take some time to write about this in your journal.

4. Reflect for a few minutes about how you might respond—in a similar way or differently—if your child makes a mistake during a task that she's already been doing for a long time, one that she already knows how to do well. Why might such mistakes happen? (For example, a sick child might soil himself even though he's been "going potty" for months. Or a child who hasn't been getting as much attention since the new sibling was born might begin to act out in order to get attention.) Notice any reactions that you have to the reasons these things happen, and write those down.

Like many parents, you'll probably develop a stronger sense of understanding and empathy when you can determine why your child behaves a certain way. You'll get better at predicting how your child will respond in certain situations, and you can plan accordingly. You can even respond differently to problem behavior, using rules and consequences based on the bigger picture. When you do this, you'll begin to see your child as more than just a collection of misbehaviors, and your relationship will improve. We hope that these things will become true for you.

In this next exercise, we'll give you an opportunity to practice using your attunement in a mindful way with your child during play. It's one thing to develop attunement to your child, and still another to learn how you might harness that attunement in an active way—in real time, so to speak. We'll give you tips about some parenting strategies to try in the context of your attunement to your child. The exercise below has been adapted from the work of Sheila Eyberg (see Hembree-Kigin and McNeal, 1995). It is one that you can—and should—practice on a daily basis with your child to help continue to develop your relationship.

EXERCISE: Play Time

Pick a time during the day that you and your child can have about ten minutes together, uninterrupted by anyone or anything else. Be sure that this time is reasonable for your whole family and that it works with eating and sleeping schedules as well as with work responsibilities (that is, homework, chores, business).

Now, during the time you've selected, play with your child—just play. She gets to direct the activity. Intervene only if she gets aggressive or destructive; otherwise, she should make the decisions. Your job is to mindfully notice what she's doing. Here are some things to do during this playtime:

- Make gentle comments about what she is doing.

- Describe and imitate what she does. For example, you might say, "You are dressing your doll—she is wearing pink." Pick up another doll and do the same.

- Praise her for appropriate behavior. Be genuine in your praise—show your pleasure in your child by smiling and making eye contact. Be specific in your praise. For example, say, "You did such a nice job of dressing your doll."

During this special playtime:

- Don't ask her questions.

- Don't give her directions.

- Don't criticize her behavior.

Each day after your ten minutes with your child, take just a little bit more time (five minutes or less) to record your thoughts and feelings about your time in your parenting journal.

Parenting Strategy: Setting Your Child Up for Success

One of the most common complaints that parents of young children have is that their children are *noncompliant*—that is, they don't follow directions. Because you ask your child to follow directions in a lot of very different situations, teaching your child how to be a "good listener" is of utmost importance. What's more, the skills we'll teach you to encourage your child to follow directions are essential to promoting good behavior in many other areas. In the following sections, we'll talk about the key components of encouraging your child to listen to and follow your directions: antecedent control, giving directions effectively, and using reinforcers.

Antecedent Control: Setting the Stage for Good Behavior

There's a saying "An ounce of prevention is worth a pound of cure." To set the stage for good behavior, it's very helpful to become aware of "setting events" for misbehavior. *Antecedent control* means thinking about what situations or triggers contribute to your child's good behavior, then structuring your interactions with your child so those factors are present. It also helps to change triggers of misbehavior. (For more on antecedents, see chapter 4.) You can think about antecedent control in a number of ways. To set the stage for our discussion of antecedent control, think about these questions and how their answers might make your child's behavior more positive or more problematic:

■ Are you and your child cheerful, well-rested, and fed, or cranky, tired, and hungry?

■ Is your child in a situation where the demands are greater than he might be able to handle, given his age and developmental maturity?

■ How's your mood and stress level in the moment? Are you feeling vulnerable or taxed? How about your child?

■ How do your expectations of your child in a given situation match the demands of the situation and what your child actually does?

■ How might the setting you and your child are in influence your child's behavior?

■ Did you give her a direction when she was engaged in a fun activity that she was unlikely to want to stop?

These questions—and their answers—can assist you in recognizing the specific things or events that may be antecedents to your child's behavior—things or events that, in other words, make certain behavior more or less likely. (They'll also give you insight into your own behavior in particular situations.) When teaching your child a new behavior or encouraging an existing behavior, it's essential that you consider these contextual features. When and how you choose to place a demand on your child, or give him a direction that you intend for him to follow, is especially critical.

Now that you've worked a bit on developing attunement to your child, and practiced specific relationship-building skills to use during play, it's time to look at contextual factors that influence your relationship. Take a few minutes to complete the following exercise. This will help you more readily recognize the contexts that influence your child's—and your own—behavior.

EXERCISE: Seeing the Whole Picture

1. Take a few moments to think about a behavior that you really want your child to do. It can be a completely new behavior or something she's already working on. Either way, it's a small goal on your course toward valued living. For example, you may want her to stay by your side in the grocery store, do her homework every night, or make a new friend at school. Write the goal that you choose for your child in your journal.

2. Now consider and write down all the steps that you would need to take to help your child achieve this goal. For example, to get her to do her homework every night, you would likely need to create a quiet place for her to work and make sure that she has all the supplies she needs in that place. You'd also need to tell her ahead of time that you will not do the work for her, but that you're available to answer questions or help her find where the answers might be. You'll probably have to make sure that she has had a break to rest from school and, because healthy food gives her brain power, a snack. As she does her homework, you'll also need to reinforce her homework-completing behavior by praising her or letting her earn rewards for sections that she's finished.

3. Now that you've considered what you'd need to do to help your child reach this goal, write down all of the steps that she'd have to take. For example, she'd need to sit at the table, read the assignment, ask for clarification (if needed), and do the work. It may be helpful to write these down in your journal.

4. Take a few moments now to read through the remainder of the exercise (steps 5–7) so you'll be able to do it with your eyes closed. You may find it helpful to read the instructions and what you have written in your journal more than once.

5. Close your eyes and picture yourself and your child doing these steps. Notice where you both are, and notice what your body postures and facial expressions look like. Become aware of your thoughts and feelings about—and any other reactions to—these steps toward your goal. If it

seems following the steps would be easy, that's great. What if following the steps isn't easy? What barriers do you face as you follow the steps?

6. Now imagine that your child really isn't doing well at meeting this goal. How do you feel about your child and her struggle to meet this goal? Picture your child in detail and imagine what this is like for her. Does she look frustrated? Do you think she feels disappointed in herself? Does she feel like a failure? What about you? Are you focused on her failure and mistakes? Do you know what's making it hard for her to succeed? Maybe there's something about this particular situation that's making it impossible to meet her goals. What might that be? Consider whether you can help her meet the goal by being more flexible with your expectations or by providing additional support.

7. In this moment, can you remember what her favorite color is or what she's good at? Take a moment to consider each of these things. Then open your eyes and write in your journal about your reactions to the various steps of this exercise.

As you work toward a goal with your child, remain mindful in the present moment so you can fully appreciate what your child experiences—the context in which he's working, his feelings, his thoughts, and so on—in trying to reach the goal. Then, with mindful awareness, adapt how you place demands on him, if that would be helpful. For example, if you'd like your first-grader to do his homework, it's important to notice whether he had a good day at school, if he's tired, if he needs a snack, and so on. By noticing these circumstances, you may alter your demands of him accordingly. Perhaps you give him thirty minutes to transition from school rather than inflexibly applying a rule about homework being started immediately when he arrives home. Or if he's frustrated with all the work he has to do, you might help him break down his homework into smaller chunks and give him breaks and encouragement in between. In this way, you accomplish your goal of ensuring that he completes his homework, but you also do it in a way that's helpful to him and that provides him with tools he can use in the future—namely, how to feel what he's feeling and still get his work done.

Parenting Strategy: Giving Directions Effectively

In addition to seeing your child's (or your own) behavior in context, one major component of teaching your child to comply with instructions is giving directions effectively. Young children often have a difficult time with directions or requests. This is because their skill of following a sequence of directions is still emerging, as is their ability to pay attention. Because of this, it can be challenging for your child to follow a string of requests, especially when you give those requests during playtime or when she's doing something else she likes to do. She'll find it even more challenging if you give directions hurriedly or if they aren't quite clear. Thus, *how* you give directions to your child is critical if you want her to follow them. Here's how to do it:

- Give one direction at a time. Giving more than that will confuse your child.

- Make your direction very clear, concrete, and specific.

- Tell your child to do the task—do not ask. If you ask, then "no" is a perfectly acceptable response.

- Be sure you have your child's attention. Say his name and establish eye contact with him.

- If you aren't sure if your child has heard you or understood the direction, have her repeat it back to you. Praise her effort in this; if elements are incorrect, clarify them for her.

- Be certain that the direction you give is something your child can already do.

- Make sure your child actually follows through with the direction to the best of his ability.

- Immediately after your child has followed your direction, praise her. If she doesn't get the job entirely correct, praise her effort and then help her complete the task to your satisfaction.

- When you praise for following directions, you may want to say something like "Thank you for your good listening."

When you give your child directions, remember the three Bs:

- Be brief.

- Be concrete.

- Be clear.

As we've mentioned before, it's critical to ensure that your child does what you have told her to do. When you're busy, it's easy to give directions quickly or in haphazard fashion and then to move on without checking to see that your directions are followed. If this happens frequently, your child unfortunately learns to *not* do what she is told, and it becomes much harder to earn her compliance. To ensure that your child follows your directions, you must learn how to effectively use rewards or "reinforcers."

Parenting Strategy: Using Reinforcers

You may remember that in chapter 4 we discussed functional analysis, a way of looking at behavior to determine the antecedents that trigger a particular behavior and the consequences that maintain it. Reinforcers, or rewards, are consequences of a particular behavior that make it more likely to happen. For example, if you give your child a lollipop each time he comes to the supermarket with you, he'll be more likely to go with you to that store quickly and without argument.

One important thing to remember about reinforcers is that they are defined by their function. If a reinforcer doesn't strengthen a particular behavior, then no matter how good it seems to you, it's not really a reinforcer. For example, we like chocolate ice cream and would be willing to work to get some. You might not like it, however, so it might not work the same way for you. Thus, it's essential to choose your reinforcers carefully, based on how they work for your child or—if you're working on changing your own behavior—for you.

One other important thing to remember is that reinforcers work best if they are small, sustainable, and delivered immediately and consistently after your child engages (or you engage) in a particular action. The next sections will give you some techniques that have been shown to encourage positive behavior.

Labeled Praise: Be Specific

One of the easiest ways of reinforcing behavior is to use *labeled praise*. Labeled praise means being very specific when you tell your child what you like about what he's doing. For example, instead of saying "Good job," you might say, "Good job setting the table." We introduced the idea of labeled praise in chapter 5, and we'll describe it in greater detail here. In early childhood, your child is just beginning to learn to manage his own behavior and to understand the consequences of his actions. Thus, it's very important to be concrete, specific, and very clear when you praise your child. Moreover, it's important to have your child's full attention: this means that timing and delivery can be everything.

Here are some helpful tips for letting your child know when you're pleased with her behavior:

■ When you praise your child, be specific: in other words, name exactly what your child did. For example, you might say, "I like how you're working on counting to ten!"

■ Ideally you'll praise your child immediately after she's performed the "target" behavior.

■ Be sure your child can hear you and that you have her attention. Say her name first to help her be attentive.

■ Make eye contact with her, if possible.

■ Be genuine—let her see and feel the joy you take in her behavior.

Read through these tips once more. Now it's your turn to try this with your child as you do the exercise below.

EXERCISE: Using Labeled Praise

1. Think about things that your child does that you'd like to see him do more frequently. For example, if your child is a toddler, using manners (like saying "please" and "thank you"), following simple directions, or sharing with playmates might be good candidates. You might also think

about what developmental tasks your child is striving to master—like holding a crayon correctly or learning her ABCs and 1-2-3s.

2. Make a list of things that your child does *sometimes* but perhaps not yet consistently. Write these down in your parenting journal.

3. Choose two or three of these behaviors, and notice when your child performs—or attempts to perform—them. Immediately say, "I like how you did X."

It's essential that you praise your child's behavior as frequently as possible. Why is it important to praise your child's behavior? First, praise can help you build a positive relationship with your child. Second, when you use praise or rewards effectively, you help your child engage in good behavior more frequently, more consistently, or with greater intensity. Some parents take issue with giving praise, and they argue that children should simply "be good" because they're supposed to be good. Others use mild threats or power assertions to encourage good behavior. They may say, for example, "If you don't do X, I'll take away your toys." The truth of the matter is, neither of these tactics is particularly effective in the long run.

Other Types of Rewards

Rewards don't have to be expensive or fancy. They should be things that are small, that your family can afford over a period of time, and that are easy to use. Each time your child engages in a behavior you appreciate, immediately give him a reward. Over time, as your child learns to behave appropriately as a habit, you may begin to "fade," or slowly spread out and discontinue, using rewards. However, be sure to plan this fading process—that is, don't allow the rewards to fade away because of some obstacle, such as poor planning or simply because you forget to give them. It's also helpful to give small, immediate rewards and then give a larger, more substantial reward after a specified period of good behavior. We'll discuss how to do that in chapter 8.

Here are some ideas for small rewards:

- Smiles

- Pats on the back or hugs

- Stickers

- Extra playtime with mom or dad

- A favorite dessert or meal

- Something that you and your child mutually decide upon

What Behaviors Should You Reward?

You may struggle with what behaviors to reward. As we've discussed in previous chapters, you may find it hard to "see the good" if your child has struggled with misbehaviors for some time. This may mean that you tend to view your child in a narrow, rigid way and notice misbehavior more frequently than good behavior. Try the exercise below to help you acknowledge and compassionately hold a more balanced view of your child.

EXERCISE: Mindfulness and Noticing the Good

Pick up your parenting journal and find the goal that you set for you and your child in the Seeing the Whole Picture exercise earlier in this chapter. Look at your reactions to her mistakes or failures. Just notice them on the pages of your journal.

Now consider your reactions when she meets goals and behaves well. Write down how your reactions are the same or different in each case.

Hopefully the last couple of exercises helped you to see your child wholly—the good, the bad, and the neutral—all in the same moment, even when things aren't going exactly as you'd hoped or planned and even when he's messing up. Being aware of your child's "being good" is perhaps most important in these times when things aren't going as you'd like. In your next interaction with your child, see if you can catch him doing the right thing, even if for just a brief moment—or see if you can notice him smiling and having fun and how that makes you feel.

Telling Your Child What You Are Up To

When you've identified some behaviors you'd like your child to do more frequently, it's sometimes a good idea to sit down with her before beginning to "encourage the good" to let her know. This can be especially useful with children nearing school age and beyond. It's also very important to ensure that the target behaviors you choose are things that your child can already do (that is, she may have done this behavior in another context or for another reason) and that your expectations of your child are developmentally appropriate. Here's an example of how to have a conversation with your child and to adapt your expectations of your child to fit her level of skill.

❧ Jillian and Picking an Outfit

Every morning Alli struggles with five-year-old Jillian about what she should wear to kindergarten. Typically Jillian insists that nothing matches, that she likes nothing, or she can't find some essential piece of clothing that's inevitably in the laundry. This process often results in tears, an emotionally charged drive to school, and frequent tardiness. The whole situation is so unpleasant, and it's hard for Alli to think of what behaviors to encourage. It's easy to think of things to stop—like the tantrums, the whining, the indecision, and the refusal to get dressed. Alli is typically so frustrated that it's also hard for her to think clearly. She just wants the situation to stop, and she has been using a lot of scolding and empty threats to accomplish this but to no avail.

Despite her frustration, Alli takes some time one afternoon to think through what to do. What she wants to see more of is Jillian quickly choosing a weather-appropriate outfit. She tries to notice situations through the day in which Jillian makes quick choices. Typically these occur when only a few options—two or three at most—are presented to Jillian. That gives Alli an idea. She sits down with Jillian one day after school. "Jilly, it seems like you're really good at making choices. That's a really big-girl thing to do. I'm so proud of you when you make choices quickly." "Thanks, Mommy," replies Jillian. "I'm especially proud of you when you make quick choices about your school clothes, because I know it's really hard for you to do that. I'm going to help you by putting out three outfits the night before. In the morning, you can choose one of the three. How does that sound?" "Can I help pick the outfits at night?" asks Jillian. "Of course!" says her mother. That night Alli and Jillian lay out three outfits. In the morning, Jillian is able to choose much more quickly than before. "Good job making a choice, Jilly," says her mother, beaming.

Using praise or other rewards as well as setting the stage for good behavior are not, however, foolproof ways to ensure that your child will behave well. They're two of a collection of strategies that, if used correctly, can be quite effective at promoting desired behavior. Used over time, these strategies can be very helpful.

Parenting Strategy: Rethinking Your Expectations by Using Shaping

So far we've discussed techniques that are useful for encouraging your child to do things that he already does. But how do you teach your child something new—something he's never done before? To do this, we recommend a procedure called *shaping*, which involves rewarding *successive approximations*, or small steps, of a complex behavior. For example, if you're teaching your child how to add sums, he must learn first to count, then to recognize quantities, then to recognize written symbols for numbers, then how addition works, and so on. Your child should be rewarded for trying each step, until that particular step is mastered. Once he masters a step, that step is no longer reinforced. Instead, his attempts at the next, harder step are rewarded until he's able to complete all the required steps of a behavior. To summarize, here are the steps for shaping behavior:

1. Identify a behavior that you would like your child to learn.

2. Break that behavior down into manageable, feasible steps.

3. Show your child how to do the first step, and when she does it, praise her.

4. Reward your child for doing each step until it's mastered—then show her how to do the next step and reward that, until she masters the desired behavior.

You may find it hard to visualize this process until you try it with your own child. Remember, however, that you've already worked on breaking down things you'd like your child to learn into goals and then breaking these goals down into smaller steps to reach them. The process of shaping is similar. The following exercise will help you break down a new, complex behavior you'd like your child to learn into manageable steps.

EXERCISE: Shaping Your Child's Behavior— and Your Own

1. Think of a new behavior that you want your child to do. Write that new behavior in your parenting journal, then take five to ten minutes to think of the different steps involved in that behavior and the order in which they need to occur. Write those steps—and the order in which they need to be taken—in your journal. Now think about ways to reward your child as he tries each step, and write those down too. You may want to share this list with your child.

2. Now do the same process for yourself. Think of the parenting behavior that would be necessary to have your child master this new behavior. Write each step you need to take in your journal. Now think about how you can reward yourself as you try each step. Write this in your journal too.

Being Attuned to Your Child's Abilities

Whether you're teaching your child something new or encouraging something he already does is an important distinction. For example, it would be counterproductive to direct your child to clean her whole room if she's never cleaned it before. If you asked this of her, she might simply ignore what you say. However, if your child already knows how to pick up her toys, it would be appropriate to expect, in most circumstances, that she do that again. So when you use shaping, it's essential to have an accurate idea of what your child can do and what she cannot do. Also keep in mind that your child is constantly developing and may learn things that surprise you. That's one reason it's important to be attuned to and aware of the full range of your child's capabilities and skills.

Shaping Your Parenting Skills

You can also use shaping with your own behavior as a parent, as you did in the exercise above. If you haven't tried a particular parenting technique before, you may find it helpful to think of learning the skill in increments. Be sure to give yourself space to make mistakes or to try a particular skill without doing it absolutely perfectly as you learn to implement it in different situations or interactions with your child. Using the skills of mindfulness and valuing here often help clarify how to do this. Practice mindfulness to cultivate a present-moment awareness and acceptance of your own imperfections and mistakes. Valuing will help you stay on course to develop and maintain a healthy, nurturing relationship with your child. Both of these skills will help you master the use of the parenting strategies we have shown you in progressively more challenging situations. For example, it's easy to practice mindful awareness and attunement to your child in a brief playtime. But what about when your child yells at you in public? If you're like most parents, situations like those send whatever effective parenting skills you have learned completely out of your head! So you might think about a hierarchy of situations—from easy to difficult—in which it is hard for you to stay attuned to your child in the present moment. Then, keeping that in mind, you might practice the skill of attunement in increasingly difficult situations until you become comfortable in each one. And, just as you have given rewards to your child when she masters a step, you should also take a few minutes to give yourself a pat on the back for your efforts and eventual success. Try the exercise below to help you to work through a situation where your mind evaluates your parenting skills negatively.

EXERCISE: Your Skills As They Are, Not As Your Mind Describes Them

You've already been considering and writing down your reactions to carrying out various steps of parenting behavior. If you're like many parents, your reactions have included a lot of judgments contributed by your mind. Take some time now to see your skills as they really are. Begin by reading the exercise through once or twice so you don't have to refer to the book.

1. Close your eyes and imagine a recent interaction with your child. If you can, picture this interaction as if you are watching a movie about your life. Watch it "from the outside" so that you can see yourself as your child would see you—leave your mind out of the picture. How are you holding

your body? What's the expression on your face? What are you saying, and what are you doing? How does your child respond to you?

2. Write down in as much detail as possible what the interaction looked like. Do not write down anything that you could not know from the outside— just write the facts about what happened.

3. Now notice how the interaction feels and how you feel about yourself as a parent. Write these feelings in your journal.

Teaching Your Child About Consequences

Many situations pull for you to be inconsistent in your parenting. But what does it mean to be consistent in your parenting? Here are the primary elements of consistency in parenting:

- Do what you say. For example, when you promise a reward, you should deliver that reward as you promised.

- When you give directions to your child, be sure that your child follows through.

- Unless some circumstances prevent this, keep your directions—and the consequences for following or not following them—the same for your child while he is at a certain developmental stage.

As we mentioned before, when you're not consistent, you set the stage for your child to ignore you. For example, if you place a demand on your child and then do something else without checking that your child has followed your direction or without praising her compliance, you set the stage for her to simply *not* do what she is told. Similarly, if you use empty threats to coerce your child into doing what you ask, your child may call your bluff and then refuse your directions. Thus, it's of utmost importance that you don't give directions that you cannot enforce. In the next section, we'll offer some tips to help you be more consistent and to help your child to understand the consequences of his behavior.

Using Contingency Statements

In order to help your child understand the consequences of his actions, use *contingency statements*: these are "If...then" statements. For example, you might say, "If you clean your room, then you can watch your favorite cartoon." Using if–then statements works particularly well with young children, whose reasoning as to why they should behave is still emerging. Their choices about what they do are contingent upon the consequences of those acts, and that understanding develops over time and with practice. For example, you might say something like "If you put your toy cars in the case, then you'll get the new race car you want." A statement phrased in this way helps your child understand that if she follows your directions, she will gain a reward. Of course, you must support such statements by consistently doing what you say.

It can be hard to think up if–then statements in the moment, especially when you have many other things going on that distract you from your interaction with your child. Similarly, you may make an if–then statement that is actually a bribe (promising a reward, or even giving one, to a child *before* he has performed the appropriate behavior) or an empty threat (describing a negative consequence for a behavior that you have no intention or ability to deliver). One rule of thumb when you come up with contingency statements is this: do what you say, exactly how you say you will. In particularly rough situations, such as when your child throws a tantrum in front of others, you'll find it hard to think of if–then statements, much less actually carry them out. At times like these, many parents just give in to their children's whims, but you don't have to do this. There are two helpful ways to prevent this from happening. First, check in with yourself about your parenting values on a regular basis. Second, create if–then statements, consistent with what you can and are willing to do with or for your child, to use before tough situations arise. Having appropriate if–then statements to draw on will allow you to use your time and energy to deal more effectively with your child's behavior.

Because coming up with contingency statements can be so difficult, use the following exercise to help you come up with a few if–then statements to use in challenging situations.

EXERCISE: When the Going Gets Tough

1. Think of a tough interaction that you and your child often have—for example, when you're standing in the checkout line at the grocery, just finishing the last bedtime story, or rushing to school in the morning. In your journal, write down what the tough interaction is and list all the things that you and your child typically do in that situation.

2. Brainstorm what you could say in that situation that would establish rules and consequences for your child. For example, "If you get out of bed by 7:30, you will get a sticker." Write down all of your ideas. Don't evaluate their practicality or potential success. Just list as many as you can. Set a timer and write for five minutes. Don't stop writing. If you get stuck, just keep writing the same idea until something new comes to your mind. This is a time when your mind is very helpful!

3. Now look at your list. Take some time to think about each idea: how likely you are to actually do it, how your child might respond to it, and if there's a better, related alternative. Narrow your list down to the reasonable, practical, and potentially successful ideas. Try to have at least two or three for your tough situation with your child. Now write out the if–then statements that express your ideas.

A Few Words on Consistency and Flexibility

While it's important for you to be consistent, it's also important to be flexible in how you parent your child. For example, if you know your child is feeling sick or tired, you might lower your expectations for her behavior a notch. By being flexible, however, we don't mean being inconsistent. Remember that being inconsistent means not doing what you say you will do or not ensuring that your child does what you say. *Flexibility* means having a set of expectations of and rules for your child, and deciding in a judicious way when, and how, to apply them. The key to this is being fully present in the moment and attuned to the context in which your child's behavior is occurring. That same context sets the stage for your parenting behavior and helps you to flexibly choose appropriate parenting strategies. Awareness of and sensitivity to context help prevent knee-jerk parenting and promote effective use of the behavior management skills we have described here. When you lose touch with the present moment, there's a risk of applying these skills in a rigid way that will not be useful to you or your child.

Summary

In this chapter, we provided guidance in building a strong relationship with your child as a foundation for encouraging good behavior. Such a relationship helps you become attuned to your child's motives and emotional states. Understanding your child in this way, in the moment, promotes sensitive and responsive parenting and supports the development of effective behavior management techniques. We also described some basic techniques that are helpful in fostering good behavior, particularly compliance. These included choosing when and how to ask your child to follow your directions, giving directions clearly and well, the use of praise and rewards, and, finally, parenting consistently, even in the face of difficult situations.

CHAPTER 8

Using ACT for Acting-Out Behaviors

Love is at the root of all healthy discipline. The desire to be loved is a powerful motivation for children to behave in ways that give their parents pleasure rather than displeasure. It may even be our own long-ago fear of losing our parents' love that now sometimes makes us uneasy about setting and maintaining limits. We're afraid we'll lose the love of our children when we don't let them have their way.

Fred Rogers

In the previous chapters, we've discussed strategies for developing a positive, responsive relationship with your child and, in that context, for encouraging good behavior. But sometimes those strategies aren't enough to curb inappropriate behavior. In this chapter, we'll discuss how to address misbehaviors that are of greater concern. We'll also give you some opportunities to apply what you have learned in previous chapters as well as what you will learn in this one.

In early childhood, some of the most common frustrations parents report include "acting-out" behaviors, such as throwing tantrums, being oppositional (refusing to follow directions), being verbally or physically aggressive, and acting without thinking, which is often called "impulsivity."

It's important to remember that all of these behaviors, in small or moderate doses, are part of normal development in young children. Yet there are a few caveats. First, allowing such behavior to continue without consistent and firm guidance can set the stage for it to escalate and interfere with academic success and friendships as well as disrupt your family relationships in middle childhood and adolescence. Second, if you feel your child's behaviors are serious, and if they disrupt your family life or his academic or social life and cause significant distress, we encourage you to seek help from a practitioner who specializes in early childhood behavioral treatments. If this does describe your situation, the skills we present in this book may help keep you motivated and focused on your values as you progress through treatment with your child.

Tantrums

Tantrums are the tempests of early childhood. All children have these "meltdowns," although some tantrums are certainly more intense and long-lived than others. Different triggers or situations influence how much and when your child throws tantrums. Because tantrums can have different "functions" for children, which simply means that they result in different consequences (see chapter 4), each tantrum might require a different parenting strategy grounded in ACT. This sometimes makes it difficult for you to know what to do in a particular situation. Therefore, we'll describe a few common triggers of tantrums as well as what to do in each situation.

Triggers and Setting Events

Tantrums can be a sign that your child is tired, cranky, and feeling overwhelmed, or that a particular situation is simply too much for her. For example, you may be overscheduled, so you must juggle numerous obligations, errands, meetings, playdates, appointments, and so on. If you bring your child with you to these various commitments, you may expect her to be patient and to handle transitions at a level far beyond her years. For example, perhaps you have a dental appointment that requires a long wait in a waiting room that doesn't have many toys or child-friendly books and activities. You might expect her mood to hold, and for her to sit still and be patient—yet all of those expectations might not be realistic for her, depending on her age. If you and your child are in a situation like this, even your small demands may be met with whining or screaming. She may even burst into tears, seemingly unexpectedly, with no provocation whatsoever. Thus, carefully consider your child's developmental level in order to more accurately determine what she can handle in a particular situation. Additionally, you'll need to think through if you should require your child—and, if so, how—to act on your directions when she finds a situation very challenging.

In situations like the one described above, your best bet is to change the situation or the triggers that might make a tantrum more likely. Here are a few tips:

Consider the situation from your child's perspective. Put yourself in your child's place and think about how particular events, or sequences of events, might affect his behavior. If you feel a particular situation lies beyond his capacity for coping, plan to break it down into smaller pieces. For example, if you must run three errands, is there a way you can take a break to grab a snack for your child after one or two of the errands? If a situation requires your child to be patient, you might bring toys, activities, or snacks that will help keep him entertained.

Notice your child's mood and physiological state. Is she emotional and tired or active and alert? Think about ways of communicating empathy for what your child is experiencing: either place smaller demands on her or increase your level of guidance to help her follow a demand. For example, if you're in a waiting-room situation and she's bored, perhaps you can loosen your expectation of her to sit still. You might allow her to run around a little. Or, if you're unwilling to do that, perhaps you could help her sit still by engaging her in a game, like "Rock, Paper, Scissors" or "I Spy," to occupy her while you both are waiting. This might make it easier for her to comply with your request or expectation for her to sit quietly. If your child is in a terrible mood, or is hungry or thirsty or tired, you might choose not to make too many requests of her while she is in this state. In other words, choose your battles carefully.

Notice how you're feeling and what you're thinking. Take a few moments to gauge how attached you are to your feelings and thoughts. Are you truly in the moment with your child, or are you more focused on other things? See if you can practice the skill of mindful awareness and bring yourself to the present moment. Full, nondefensive acceptance and awareness of the situation will help you place demands (or resist giving them!) in a sensitive, responsive manner.

Ask yourself if you're ignoring your child. Have you been so focused on something else that you've ignored—perhaps repeatedly—your child's bids for attention? Sometimes children throw tantrums if tantrums gained their parents' attention in the past. Could this be happening with your child? If so, practice mindfully noticing your child's good behavior and praising her for behaving well.

Notice the timing and content of your direction or demand. Have you just given your child a direction or asked him to do something he'd rather not do? If he throws a tantrum right after this, he probably expects you to remove your direction or demand. If this is the case, give some thought to how you typically handle this situation. We'll come back to situations like this in a moment in greater detail.

Notice if you've set a limit or denied a request. When you set a limit on your child's behavior or refuse her request, does she throw a tantrum? If so, do you give in to your child or stick to what you say? Giving in promotes more tantrums in the long run. Consider how you typically handle this situation.

The situations we described above are very typical contexts that tend to trigger tantrums in children. Becoming aware of and altering these triggers can help make tantrums less likely. Work through the following mindfulness exercise to brainstorm how you might plan for situations in which tantrums are likely to occur.

> ### EXERCISE: Planning for Tantrums and Other Disruptive Behaviors

It's important to consider that every child is different, and every moment with your child has unique characteristics that make problem behavior more or less likely. There's no way to plan for all situations. However, you—as the expert on your child's behavior—are likely to know what things typically "set him off." To help you be aware of such triggers, consider the following and write your answers in your journal:

- The places that my child acts out the most are…

- The time of day (or night) that my child's behavior concerns me the most is…

- The activities that seem to most relate to my child's misbehavior are…

- Just before my child throws a tantrum or otherwise acts out, my mood is usually…

- Just before my child throws a tantrum or otherwise acts out, I usually have…

Hopefully answering these questions has given you some understanding of what is going on for your child and has allowed you to take her perspective in an empathetic way so that you can feel as she does. Your answers may also have given you some clues about the function of your child's behavior. When you know why your child is doing a certain behavior, which is usually either to get something or get out of something, you can change the situation so that you prevent that need. You can also change what happens after the behavior (the consequence), but right now we're focusing on adapting the context so that problems aren't triggered.

Take some time now to consider ways that you can do this for your child. Make a list in your journal. Your list might include being mindful about your own mood and about your values, or changing the tone of your voice when you give your child a command, or asking questions about what your child needs to succeed in that moment. In any case, you can probably make an observable change that will help the situation from becoming a trigger for acting out. Think about how you could shift the context, then write about that in as much detail as possible.

Unhelpful Consequences

Consequences are events that happen as a result of our behavior (see chapter 4). Even when you change the context through carefully minimizing triggers, you might change your own behavior in unhelpful ways if your child does begin to throw a tantrum. This is called *changing consequences*, or changing your own parenting strategy as a result of your child's behavior, for tantrums. In the section above, we mentioned two situations—tantrums occurring after a demand is placed (after you tell your child to do something) and tantrums that happen after you set a limit (telling your child no, for example). After tantrums begin in these situations, you might be tempted to remove the demands you set or to give in to your child. When there are situational constraints—for example, if you're in a hurry and your child's tantrum slows you down, or you're in a public place and a tantrum leaves you highly embarrassed—you may be even more likely to give in. Unfortunately when you do this, it can inadvertently reinforce the tantrum. Simply put, it teaches your child that tantrums *work*. When something works, your child will use it more often. Consider the example below.

❧ Ending the Playdate

Seema had taken Samir, her four-year-old son, to a playdate at a neighbor's house. The children were having fun, and Seema and her neighbor had a cup of coffee together and chatted. After a time, Seema realized that the day had slipped by and that she was going to be late for an important appointment. "Samir! Goodness, we have to go. Five more minutes and then you need to say good-bye to your friend!" Samir looked at her angrily. "But we're playing a game! NO! I don't want to go!" He ran out of the playroom and to his friend's bedroom. Seema hurriedly excused herself and ran after him. "Samir. Come ON. We have to go! Mommy will be late!" "I DON'T CARE! I'm NOT going!" her son said. After continuing to argue and trying to convince Samir to come with her of his own accord, Seema gave up. "Fine. You can have ten more minutes. AND THEN WE ARE GOING." When ten more minutes had passed, Samir refused again. Seema's friend offered to watch him so that Seema could go to her appointment and then pick him up later. Seema agreed, and Samir stayed to play with his friend. Seema was both furious with him and relieved that she could go and not have to worry about it anymore. She was also sheepish and embarrassed that Samir had displayed such bad behavior in front of her friend. She wondered if he would be invited over ever again.

EXERCISE: How Could the Consequences Be Different?

Consider Seema and how things worked out for her. She did do some things that would likely prevent problem behavior. For example, she gave Samir playtime with his friend, and she gave him a five-minute warning prior to them needing to leave. Unfortunately those things didn't work. She also followed him immediately after he ran from her, which is important in terms of ensuring that he followed through on her direction. However, when she went after him—rather than repeating her direction or providing appropriate punishment for his misbehavior—Seema began to argue with Samir. The situation escalated, and Seema, in addition to becoming even more late for her appointment, was embarrassed. So she gave up and did not follow through with her demand for Samir to leave with her.

Consider each of the following and write your answers in your parenting journal:

1. What do you think might have been different if Seema had talked, or even role-played, with Samir about the end of the playdate before they got to their friends' house?

2. Remember that it's important to consider whether or not your child is capable of behaving appropriately in a certain situation. You need to think about his age, whether the behavioral skills needed have been learned, and what else might set him up for success or failure. What if Seema had expected a tantrum to start, given her child's abilities or mood, and was therefore able to be calmer in the situation? What if she had talked to the other mother about how it might get bad? Might she have been able to redirect Samir by giving him something fun to do in the car, for example? What would you think and how would you feel if you were in a similar situation?

3. What other ideas do you have about what Seema could have done? Remember that if your child stops a tantrum or other misbehavior, even just briefly, you should reinforce that behavior.

Parenting Strategy: Using Planned Ignoring with Tantrums

We mentioned earlier that when you remove your demand because your child throws a tantrum, you may actually make tantrums more likely to occur. The same is true when you set limits. When you set a limit with your child and she begins to whine or throw a tantrum, it may be because she expects you to loosen or remove that limit. If this is the case, the most effective thing to do is to maintain the limit that you have set and to use planned ignoring. We introduced this strategy in chapter 6 and will review how to use it more specifically with tantrums here.

Planned ignoring means removing your attention from your child in very specific situations—that is, when he's misbehaving. When your child throws a tantrum, especially after you've set a limit, it's helpful to do the following:

1. If your child is between three and five years old, say, "I will play with you as soon as you are done yelling [screaming or whatever]." If your child is older than five, you might say, "If you need space to yell, go to your room. You're welcome to come out when you're done."

2. After you've said this, get busy doing something else. If your child is younger, it may be helpful to do some subtle supervision to ensure that he doesn't escalate to throw objects or hit anyone else in the family.

3.   As soon as your child stops her tantrum, go to her and say, "Nice work calming yourself down." You may choose to help her engage in an activity afterward to help her make this transition as well as to communicate to her your attention to her positive behavior.

4.   After the tantrum stops, acknowledge how hard it was for your child to experience the limit you set and to assert that when you set a limit, you mean it. For example, you might say, "I know you don't like it when I say no to things. But when I say no, that means no, no matter how upset you get or how loud you yell at me."

To consider how you might handle a similar situation involving a tantrum that occurs when you set a limit, work through the exercise below.

EXERCISE: Willingness and Problem Solving

You can do this exercise now in your imagination so that you can be prepared for your child's next tantrum or other misbehavior. It involves three elements: (1) a mindful noticing of antecedents (triggers) and consequences that are relevant to your child's behavior; (2) your awareness of your own willingness to feel whatever you feel, and (3) your commitment to parent consistently despite your feelings.

1.   Take a moment to recall a situation in which your child threw a tantrum. As best you can, try to place yourself back into that situation. Where does this occur? What's going on around you? What are the triggers for the tantrum? How are you feeling in that moment? Can you recall any thoughts? Do you try to intervene? What happens? What are the consequences of your actions? See if you can notice, without evaluation or judgment, all of your reactions when things go differently than planned, especially when you have planned for prevention.

2.   Now let those reactions go from your mind and concentrate on the kind of parent that you want to be and on what "that" parent would do in this moment. What would you say? What might you do differently?

3.   If you notice yourself getting distracted or hooked by unpleasant thoughts and feelings, gently acknowledge them and bring yourself back to the task at hand. This experience of getting "hooked" by your thoughts is likely very similar to what may actually happen when you're in an actual

situation when your child throws a tantrum. Learning how to tell when you are in—and out of—the present moment and how to bring yourself back to task are critical to effectively intervening when your child throws a tantrum.

4. Write down your responses in your parenting journal. The next time your child throws a tantrum, try to implement the strategies you have devised here. Notice any differences in how you experience your child's tantrum—in other words, if it *feels* different to you in the moment. Also notice whether the parenting strategies you have come up with in this exercise work differently from those you have tried before.

Being Stubborn (or Oppositional)

Being oppositional, which is a way of saying "being stubborn," is a hallmark of early childhood. It heralds your child's developing autonomy and independence. However, it can also be incredibly frustrating when you give your child a direction and he refuses to follow it. This is especially important in situations when your child's safety might be at risk—for example, when you tell him to look both ways before crossing the street. Thus, it is essential to teach children to comply with your directions. We'll provide a parenting strategy called "compliance training" to help you deal with oppositional behavior. In a chapter 7, we introduced ideas of how to encourage good behavior through antecedent control and giving consequences for behavior. Here we'll introduce you to a technique called "compliance training" that will help prevent or deter your child from ignoring your requests and directions.

Triggers and Setting Events

Being oppositional, by definition, happens after you ask or tell your child to do something. Situations that are more likely to elicit stubbornness vary. Interrupting your child's play, giving a direction when she's tired or cranky (or when you're tired or irritable), or giving a challenging direction that may be beyond his ability in the moment can trigger this behavior. You won't be surprised that these triggers are quite similar to those that elicit tantrums. Very often, tantrums may have the same function as noncompliance: to resist complying with demands or requests.

Unhelpful Consequences

There are many reasons that your child may not follow your directions. If, for example, you have a history of giving directions without making sure your child follows through, she may simply be used to ignoring them. This is often the case if you don't give consequences for her repeated failure to listen to you.

Parenting Strategy: Using Compliance Training

Compliance training involves helping to build some momentum in your child such that he'll be more likely to follow your directions. It's a way to get him "used to" listening in easier situations so that he'll also listen in more difficult situations—that is, those in which he's been less likely to listen in the past. To start compliance training with your child, try the following:

- Choose two or three five- to ten-minute periods during the day when you're able to focus fully on your child.

- Try to engage with your child in whatever activity he's doing. Play is an ideal situation, but there may be others, such as having your child be a "helper," which is something that young children often enjoy.

- Choose very simple directions that you can give your child that fit in the context of the ongoing activity. For example, if your child is playing, you might ask him to hand you a particular toy, or give you a turn, or tell you something about what he's doing. If your child is helping you, you might ask him to bring you something or to run a quick, simple errand. Try to choose things that your child both enjoys doing and is highly likely to want to do.

- When you have six to eight simple, easy-to-follow directions that you can give to your child, go ahead and give them. Pay attention to how you say them (see chapter 7), and give them one at a time, one after another. After your child completes each request, praise him and give the next direction. After he completes the string of directions, use labeled praise (see chapter 7) to reward him for his "good listening."

If you practice this simple technique over time, your child will get in the habit of following your directions. He'll also have had the experience of getting praise from you consistently as a consequence for doing what he's told. At that point, you can begin giving directions that are more difficult to follow with greater success. Work through the following exercise to see how to develop opportunities for compliance training with your child.

EXERCISE: Getting Started on Compliance Training

If you start to have reservations about when you might set aside such special time to help your child practice following directions, or about whether it will work, review who you want to be and what you want to do with respect to your child. You have thought about this a lot by now and even written it in several places in your journal. We ask you to concentrate on your parenting values in whatever way makes them feel most present to you—reading what you have written, imagining playing with your child, or doing a mindfulness exercise. Now make a commitment to get started on compliance training.

Write down in your journal what compliance training will look like for you and your child: When will you do it? What sorts of directions will you give? How will you say them? How will you get and keep your child's attention? How will you praise your child for following directions? Remember that compliance training in relatively easy situations gets children ready for following instructions in more difficult situations, such as when your child is aggressive.

Aggression

Although aggression can seem like a very serious issue, most children show either verbal or physical aggression at some point in early childhood. As they age, children become less likely to be physically aggressive and instead may show verbal aggression. For girls and some boys, it can also develop later into what is called *relational aggression*, or attempts to harm others, usually peers, through exclusion, starting rumors, or name-calling. While these behaviors are all concerning, it's important to remember that if they occur infrequently, they are fairly typical. If aggression is frequent, is intense, or consistently disrupts family routines or peer relationships, we encourage you to talk with a psychologist who can support you as you use appropriate parenting strategies to constructively deal with this behavior. Aggression is a very important issue to address in early childhood, because left untreated it may lead to other difficulties later, including problems making and keeping friends, learning social skills, and getting along in school.

Even when your child shows aggression infrequently, it's important to set firm and clear limits on this behavior. And while we have described a number of tips for promoting appropriate behavior, it's also important to learn how to give negative consequences to prevent misbehaviors like aggression. Nonetheless, it's sometimes helpful to think of aggressive behavior as arising because your child may need additional support in learning more appropriate behavior to get her needs met. Thus, we'll discuss common situations in which aggression may arise, provide strategies for encouraging more appropriate alternative behaviors, and describe how to deliver consequences to stop aggression.

Triggers and Setting Events

When your child acts aggressively—whether toward you or toward peers—it's important to understand the context in which this behavior arises. Consider the following situations that sometimes elicit aggression in young children. Aggression may be a response to

- placing demands;

- setting limits;

- a perceived slight or unfairness, such as when someone takes a toy away; or

- frustration.

These are just a few common triggers of aggression in young children. You may observe many other situations that might trigger verbal or physical aggressive behavior in your child.

Unhelpful Consequences

Just like any other behavior, when aggression works for your child, it's more likely to continue. Thus, it's important to consider the function and consequences of aggression. Ask yourself these questions:

- What does aggression do for my child?

- What happens as a result of my child's aggression?

143

If there aren't clear negative consequences for aggressive behavior—if, for example, playground bullying goes unnoticed and a child gets what he wants through this behavior, it will tend to continue. Similarly, if consequences are delivered inconsistently, this too can make it hard to change aggression.

If your child shows occasional aggressive behavior—toward you or other adults in the family, siblings, or peers—take a few moments to read the story below and then go through the exercise after the story.

Blowing Up—Out of Nowhere?

Kenny has three children: twin girls who are three and a boy who is five years old. Kenny works about forty hours a week; his office is in the family's basement. His wife is a student who also works full-time outside of their home, so Kenny does most of the day-to-day parenting tasks. He's home with all three children all day and admits he's very frustrated. Almost every day his son hits at least one of the girls, and Kenny repeatedly corrects him for yelling and throwing toys at them. Kenny sees the girls crying and gets very upset. He then yells at his son, "WHY did you throw that at her?" or "You should not hit a girl," or "She's younger and smaller than you. What is your problem?!" Kenny is so busy and stressed out that he has no idea that the twins taunt their brother and take his toys. Kenny also does not realize that, since he's often on the computer working, his son does not get much attention from him unless there is trouble.

You can probably easily see why Kenny's son acts aggressively toward his sisters. Notice how apparent the relevant contextual factors are when you aren't involved in the situation. And yet it's very likely that you've been in Kenny's place—feeling like your child has just blown up out of nowhere for no reason! When you're in the midst of your child's aggression, seeing the reason for it can be quite difficult.

EXERCISE: Dealing with Agression

1. Take a few minutes now to let yourself experience what Kenny experiences—the confusion, frustration, guilt, and whatever else is there.

2. Now, in your imagination, bring yourself back to a situation in which your child acted with aggression. To the best of your ability, put yourself back in that situation—recall what was going on around you, what you said, what you heard, and what you felt. Consider what happened just before and after the aggression. See if you can pick out important factors. You'll need your mindfulness skills for this: slow down, let go of judgments, and see what shows up.

3. Let your parenting values be present in this moment of your child's aggressive behavior too: Do you want to see her as more than her hitting? Based on your own practice of acceptance and mindfulness of difficult emotions, what coping skills might you want to share with her? What consequences might you provide for her, from that mindful, value-consistent "place"? Write down your thoughts in your parenting journal. Keep them in mind for situations that trigger aggression in your child.

Parenting Strategy: Earning Privileges—Creating a Token Economy

Just as it's important to give consequences for aggression, it's even more important to provide incentives for children to use other ways to communicate and get their needs met. This isn't the first strategy you may think of in the moment, however, as your main goal in dealing with aggression is to get it to stop. And building incentive programs for more appropriate social behavior *does* take time and effort. However, it's often time well spent. One very useful tool for providing incentives for appropriate social behavior is called a "token economy."

What a Token Economy Is and How It Works

Simply put, a *token economy* is a system in which your child earns a "token" when he engages in a desired behavior. He can then trade that token in for an actual reward. Money, for example, is a token for you—it can be traded in for all sorts of pleasant things that you're willing to work for. Thus money, while inherently just paper with printed numbers, comes to mean something very important to you by its association with rewards. Tokens function the same way for children.

Here are a few key considerations to effectively set up a token economy and make it work:

Small, immediate rewards work better than large ones that are delayed. When you set up your token system, make sure your child is able to earn tokens immediately after showing you the behavior you want to reward.

It's critical to know what your child can and cannot do. If you create a token system in which it's too difficult for your child to earn rewards, the system won't work very well. Similarly, if you make it too easy, the rewards will lose their meaning for your child. Thus, notice how often your child does a particular desired behavior and plan to give her a token for doing it slightly more frequently. For example, if your child says "please" five out of ten times when making requests of you, you might give her a token for saying "please" six or seven times, to encourage her to do it more frequently.

Determine how many tokens your child must earn to trade in for a larger reward. If your child is younger, it's important to reward him more frequently—for example, at the end of each playdate, at the end of the day, or perhaps even at the end of the morning. Older children can wait three to five days before gaining their bigger reward.

Decide which behaviors you will reward. What behaviors should you reward, especially in the context of reducing aggression? Acceptance of frustration is a good one: in situations in which your child tends to blow up and become verbally or physically aggressive, give a token for speaking politely or simply *not* showing aggression in the face of strong emotion. Expressing emotions using words, or waiting to discuss how one feels until after the surge of anger or frustration has passed are also excellent candidates. They are, however, very hard for a child this age to do—and often very hard for adults to do as well, as you know from working through some of our experiential parenting exercises in previous chapters!

For tokens, choose something that's significant to your child and feasible for you. By feasible, we mean easy to remember, portable, and easy to deliver. Stickers or bingo chips work well. Some parents use things like marbles that are kept in a jar; this is a nice idea especially for younger children, when being concrete is very important. It can be helpful to keep tokens visible—for example, on a chart on the refrigerator so your child can see how much she's earning.

Choose rewards in a collaborative discussion with your child. If your child is younger (two to four years old), have a list of rewards from which your child can choose something. If you don't give your child a list, he may come up with rewards that are too large, expensive, or time-consuming (for example, being taken to the park for several hours each time he behaves as you wish)—in other words, not sustainable. This can lead to arguments, so providing a list can streamline this conversation. With older children (five to eight years old), it's a bit easier to brainstorm together. You should try the strategy that works best with your family and your child's developmental level. Just as some general ideas, depending on your child's age, you might consider rewards that are "things"—like a new doll, book, or car—or activities—like blowing bubbles with Mom, going to get ice cream and bringing along a friend, getting to sleep outside (or in the living room) in a tent, or playing an extra thirty minutes with a video game.

One good general tip for making token economies go smoothly is to explain in child-friendly words what will be expected of you as well as of your child. For example, if you have a child age two through five years, you might say, "Mommy is going to be watching you at lunchtime all week to see if you use your big-boy words instead of whining. That's something that I'm going to do for you, and when I hear you using your words during all of lunchtime, it's my job to give you a sticker. You can pick whatever stickers you want, okay? But Mommy has to give the sticker to you when you use your words. When you get three stickers, no matter what day it is, then Mommy will give you a prize. You know the puzzle you picked out? Well, when you earn three stickers for using your big-boy words at lunch, Mommy will give you the puzzle! Do you understand? Tell me how it will work." Be enthusiastic when explaining the system. That will excite your child and help raise your energy level too.

Some Obstacles to Using Token Systems

As you might guess, token economies can be unwieldy and time-consuming to set up. Your child may not understand exactly how they work (especially if your child is younger) without some initial explaining and then repeated reminders. Additionally, sometimes rewards stop working as "rewards." This might happen if your child gets too many—too much of a good thing is sometimes unhelpful—or if she becomes bored with the reward for some other reason. One way around this is to change the rewards once in a while or to offer a choice of a "surprise" reward that is something you are fairly certain your child will enjoy.

Please work through the following exercise to explore possible obstacles for you in implementing a token economy with your child.

EXERCISE: Wow, This Is Hard!

If you've never used a token economy before and never seen how well it can work, and even if you have used one and seen it work wonders, you might be thinking that it sounds like a difficult, complicated, risky thing to try. It is—thank your mind for looking out for you, and then take a moment to consider that being a compassionate and effective parent means being willing to do hard things and to make some mistakes. One way to make the use of a token economy more successful is to brainstorm problems and solutions ahead of time.

1. In your journal, describe all of your thoughts, feelings, and other reactions to using a token economy. If you have reservations, write them down. For example, you may be thinking, *In order for this to work, I will have to watch her ALL the time—otherwise I might miss her doing the behavior I want, and she might not tell the truth about it.* You also may feel so tired that you just don't want to take the energy to devise a system, explain it, and follow through. Some parents say things like "That used to work for my child, but it quit working" or "He won't care about that."

2. Now consider how you could address each of your reservations. For example, you might focus on being mindful, allowing yourself to be human, and giving yourself permission to miss some instances of good behavior. Catching her being good and praising her most of the time (if not all the time) will work. Knowing that you may have to continually ask your child about what he likes or wants and then change rewards accordingly may also help with some frustrations, as we have described above.

3. Take a few moments now to let your awareness shift to what you hope for with respect to your child. Consider your willingness to do hard work in the service of those values. Write down your reactions in your journal.

Parenting Strategy: Using Time-Out

Now that we've discussed how to set up a more structured incentive program for encouraging appropriate social behavior, we'll describe "time-out," a very effective way to curb inappropriate behaviors that are maintained by the attention of others.

What a Time-Out Is and How It Works

Time-out is a procedure for stopping or reducing misbehavior. When a child does something inappropriate, such as breaking a "no hitting" rule, he is firmly told that the consequence for his behavior is time-out. Immediately he typically goes, or is brought to, a quiet area. While in time-out, he has no access to social reinforcers—play, attention, or camaraderie. He also should have no access to toys or other things to distract or entertain him. In short, time-out is, and should be, boring. After a short period of time, typically several minutes (one minute per year of the child's age is a good guideline), the child is invited to leave time-out and welcomed back into ongoing activities. Typically it's helpful to praise him for taking his time-out well and to remind him that time-out will be the consequence should he break the same rule again.

Ten Steps to Effective Time-Outs

Many parents use time-out incorrectly and inconsistently. This is due in part to some logistical issues that arise when planning how to use it. It can also seem a little complicated as you first get started, so we have broken it down into clear steps below. After you read the ten steps, we'll take a closer look at each one.

1. Clearly define what behaviors will result in time-out.

2. Choose an appropriate place for time-out.

3. Never implement time-out in anger.

4. When your child shows the prohibited behavior, give one warning.

5. If the rule is broken again, your child must go to time-out.

6. Use a timer, if at all possible, and keep time-outs brief.

7. Do not talk to, look at, argue with, or scold your child while your child is in time-out.

8. Reset the timer if your child leaves time-out.

9. When time-out is over, it's over.

10. Sometimes it's useful to help your child get back into ongoing activities.

By following these ten steps, you'll create an effective time-out for your child. Now let's take that closer look at each step below.

1 Clearly define what behaviors will result in time-out. Make the contingency a clear rule: if you do X, you will go to time-out. Ensure that your child knows and understands the rule, and make sure that conversation happens at a time when you both are calm and can hear and understand each other.

2 Choose an appropriate place for time-out. The bottom step of a stairway is a good choice for younger children. Hallways are also good, because there's not typically a lot of "stuff" that will serve as distraction in a hallway. Some parents simply use a chair that's in a relatively uncluttered, uninteresting spot. The spot should be boring—without a lot of toys or other entertainments (like TV) around. Use this place consistently for time-out, unless you and your child are out running errands or pursuing other activities. Ideally you should plan for a place for time-out wherever you go so your child can become familiar with those locations when he's not upset. For example, it's helpful to think through whether you might bring your child outside a shop for a time-out or whether you're comfortable plunking him down in a grocery aisle. If you're in an unfamiliar place, keep in mind that finding a spot quickly is critical. When this is not possible, you might consider an alternate consequence, such as cutting your errand short or restricting a fun activity.

3 Never implement time-out in anger. Try to be as "matter-of-fact" as possible when you use this strategy. It's certainly okay to feel angry—don't struggle with that. But in terms of your behavior, keep your voice calm and steady.

4 When your child shows the prohibited behavior, give one warning. A warning signal helps make a solid connection for the child between the behavior and the consequence. Be very clear about what will happen next if your child does the behavior again. "If–then" statements are very useful here. You might say, "Spitting at your brother is not okay. If you do that again, you will go to time-out." This will give her a chance to self-correct her behavior. This can be helpful in terms of teaching your child skills to manage her own behavior.

5 If the rule is broken again, your child must go to time-out. You may, for example, calmly state, "You used your outside voice, so you're going to time-out." Then escort him, if necessary, to the time-out spot. Do it immediately after the misbehavior has occurred and remember not to threaten time-out without following through. This consequence must be applied consistently and immediately after the child does the unwanted behavior. If your child is younger (two to four years old), it's appropriate to pick him up and bring him to time-out. If your child is older, allow him to go by himself.

6 Use a timer, if at all possible, and keep time-outs brief. One minute per year of your child's age is a good rule of thumb. Your child may sometimes throw tantrums while in time-out. You may choose to wait until she's quiet before setting your timer for the allotted time or simply to ignore the tantrum and set it immediately. Either way, be sure to use your mindfulness and planned ignoring skills. Notice her screams and pulls for your attention without judging them; let them pass by like clouds and purposefully direct your attention elsewhere.

7 Do not talk to, look at, argue with, or scold your child while your child is in time-out. Interacting with your child during time-out will ruin its effect. Also be sure that he can't see the television and that he doesn't have toys to play with.

8 Reset the timer if your child leaves time-out. Bring her back if necessary, but don't make a big deal about it. Simply take her, without making eye contact and without saying much, if anything at all. However, you might say, "Your time-out is not over yet. You go back until the time is up."

9 When time-out is over, it's over. Do not add additional punishment or scold your child afterward. Simply let him know that when rules are broken, he will experience consequences. A gentle reminder about expected behavior is effective, such as "Remember to use your inside voice" or "Remember not to spit."

> 10 Sometimes it's useful to help your child get back into ongoing activities. She may feel sheepish or embarrassed when given a time-out. Therefore, you can teach her a valuable skill by helping her to both have her emotions and re-engage in desired activities.
>
> Much like using a token economy, the proper use of time-out can be hard. It's a simple idea, but it can take a lot of effort. Being calm and consistent and refraining from arguing and pleading during the use of time-out is more easily said than done. You can, however, practice and learn these skills in preparation for situations when you'll need to use them with your child. And as we've mentioned before, keeping yourself grounded in your parenting values will also help you to be more committed to effectively using time-outs.

Summary

In this chapter, we described how to use ACT and effective parenting strategies to help you deal with "acting out" behaviors, including tantrums, opposition to rules and directions, and aggression. Although some of these strategies have been introduced in previous chapters, we provided a number of opportunities for you to think through how to use them with your own child, in ways that work best for you and your family. We talked about how to identify triggers and consequences of your child's behavior. We also showed you how to choose your battles by really noticing and changing your child's triggers. We also discussed how to reward good behavior and limit misbehavior by giving different types of consequences. Finally, we illustrated how to use more advanced strategies like a token economy and time-out. In the next chapter, we'll discuss strategies to use—and how to use them—when addressing your child's worries, fears, and avoidance.

CHAPTER 9

Supporting Your Anxious Child

*It's not only children who grow. Parents do too. As much as
we watch to see what our children do with their lives, they are
watching us to see what we do with ours. I can't tell my children
to reach for the sun. All I can do is reach for it myself.*

Joyce Maynard

So far, we've mostly discussed how to use ACT-based skills in dealing with disruptive behaviors in your young child—things like stubbornness, arguing, and not following directions. Some children, however, may struggle with worries and fears. They may have a more reserved temperament and be quieter and less adventurous than other children. Perhaps your child clings to you in unfamiliar places or situations or is extremely shy. Or maybe your child has a low threshold for becoming fearful and then is adamant about avoiding those things, people, or situations that arouse his anxiety. You might have a hard time knowing what to do with these behaviors—for example, should you soothe and comfort your child? Should you encourage him to experience feared situations or allow him to avoid them? If you encourage him to face his fears, will that somehow harm him? And what about how *you're* feeling when your child expresses how vulnerable he feels when he's afraid?

In this chapter, we'll discuss times when your young child's worries and fears can get in the way and what, from an ACT perspective, you can do to help. To begin, consider the following story.

✤ Abby and Her Mom

"Mom, I don't want you to go. Please stay here! What if something happens?" Abby says. "Honey, it will be okay," her mother replies. "What are you worried about?

I'll be back soon. We're just going to dinner." "But Mom! Please! I don't like it when you are away! What if something happens? I won't know where you are!" Abby pleads. "Abby, I am going out. It's going to be okay! You can always call on my cell," says her mother. "But MOM!" Abby is now red-faced, and her eyes have grown red as she hops up and down and wrings her hands. "MOM. PLEASE. I get REALLY scared when you're gone, and I don't like to have that feeling! PLEASE don't go. PLEASE!"

Abby's mother is torn. On one hand, she thinks, Poor Abby, she looks so worried, and her little body is so tense. On the other, this thought flashes across her mind with a pang of irritation: But what is the big deal? Why can't she just let it go? Why can't I ever just go out without this exhausting drama all the time? That thought is immediately followed by another: I'm being so selfish. I should be there for her. What kind of awful mother has these thoughts?

Abby's mother doesn't know what to do. She knows that Abby eventually will need to separate from her and develop independence, but she worries about pushing her daughter too hard too soon. And while she also feels as if she needs and deserves "away time," Abby's mom is concerned about whether this is the right time. It feels wrong to go, and it feels not quite right to stay either. She sighs and feels trapped.

You, Your Child, and Anxiety

Have you ever felt this way about your child's anxiety and related behavior? If so, you are certainly not alone—and neither is your child. Some parents respond to their child's strong feelings with frustration, while others try to soothe away their child's fears. It's a difficult task to appreciate your child's intense feelings—especially if they make you uncomfortable—and make a space for them to be expressed. Like many parents, you may treat your child's worries as problems to be solved or as challenges to be avoided. It's important to understand that anxiety is a natural and necessary emotion that we experience whether we want to or not. All children—all humans, really—experience worries and fears. Anxiety in and of itself is a normal human experience that involves emotions, thoughts, and sensations. Sometimes your child might experience anxiety in a positive way—for example, if she's nervously anticipating a party or other fun event. On the other hand, sometimes she might experience anxiety as unpleasant—for instance, when she worries that she's made an error at school or when she's nervous about seeing a threatening-looking dog during a neighborhood walk. It's this unpleasant experience of anxiety that may seem more common and more worrisome. However, even this type of worry or fear is just part of life.

When your child feels anxious and this begins to interfere with his functioning in school, with friends, or in the context of family routines, this may concern you as a parent. Likewise, when you're feeling anxious—perhaps about your child, your parenting, or some other stressor—you may find that your anxiety interferes with your own functioning. Let's look more closely now at early childhood worries and fears, how to support your anxious child, and how to use ACT strategies to become more mindful and accepting of your own anxiety in the service of being a compassionate and effective parent.

What Are Fears, Anxieties, and Worries?

When we talk about how to address your child's anxiety, a useful place to start is with understanding fear. *Fear* is simply a reaction to a real or perceived danger or threat. As we mentioned earlier, it involves bodily sensations, thoughts, and feelings. Fear happens when your child's *sympathetic nervous system* (which controls the fight-or-flight response) "revs up" to mobilize her body to respond to a perceived danger. This part of fear happens quickly and without any thought. And there are some really good reasons for this. For example, if your child saw a frightening dog running toward her, she'd likely experience a rapid increase in heart rate, a feeling of muscular tension, quickening of her breath, and tingling in her hands and legs. She might also notice her attention narrowing so that she only notices the dog as it approaches. Everything else going on around her is, or seems, irrelevant in comparison to this danger. All of this happens so that she can quickly jump out of harm's way. There's no thinking involved because, in a situation like this, her body needs to be ready to simply react—and fast! Once the threat has passed, however, her *parasympathetic nervous system* helps bring back equilibrium by returning her body to its resting state.

Anxious Feelings and Behavioral Avoidance

Unlike fear, *anxiety* typically refers to a sense of unease associated with anticipation of danger. We think of anxiety in terms of two things: anxious thoughts and feelings, and avoidance of situations or things that one is anxious about. This avoidance can be of places or external things, but it can also include avoiding thoughts, feelings, or other internal events. In fact, *worrying*, or turning anxiety-provoking thoughts over and over in your head in the absence of any real danger, is one form of avoiding your experience. Some people feel that ruminating about "what ifs" makes those potentialities somehow more controllable or preventable. However, worry has been shown to *prevent* people from coping well with their anxiety in an accepting way. For example, if you're too involved with your worries, your attention is taken away from other, potentially pleasant things going on around you.

As you might guess, anxiety varies a lot among people and even varies across time and situations. How anxious your child is about a particular event has a little to do with his temperament and a lot to do with what he's learned. Some children have lower thresholds than others for becoming anxious; these lower thresholds are, in part, simply a reflection of how they are "built." Another big part of anxiety has to do with what your child has experienced, as well as how she sees you react to your own fears—and to hers. Children learn many things—anxiety included—through direct experience and through watching others. For example, if your child sees you avoid or react fearfully to a spider, she may learn to be hesitant around spiders as well. How intensely your child experiences anxiety is also related to the meanings she attributes to the feared event, her anxiety itself, or both. But this is only part of the story. Sometimes when children experience anxiety, they avoid feared situations. Although this relieves their distress and may make them feel better in the short run, in the long run it may spread to other situations and keep them from doing things that, or from being with people who, are important to them. Here's a brief story to illustrate.

❧ Linus Needs Reassurance

Linus is an eight-year-old boy whose parents describe him as a worrier. He's always been rigid in terms of schedules: needing to know what's going to happen next, where his parents are going and when they'll return, or when he'll be picked up from school. He gets very upset when his schedule is disrupted or something happens that is inconsistent with what he's been told. Once his mother was fifteen minutes late picking him up from school, and according to the school counselor, he was inconsolable. He couldn't say why. He asks for a lot of reassurance around all of these issues, and sometimes he gets very stubborn and argumentative when he doesn't feel reassured. Linus is also scared of the dark. He insists on having the light on and his door open when he goes to sleep. His parents have to do a very specific bedtime ritual with him, where they must read three stories, kiss him on each cheek, and tuck him in. His parents often feel that they must accommodate these requests because if they don't, Linus throws a tantrum and refuses to go to bed. It's gotten to the point that Linus is unable to go to sleep on his own in his own room. He also doesn't go on sleepovers to friends' homes, as he's not comfortable without his parents there. As a result, he feels sad and lonely, and he has few friends. His parents just don't know what to do—they feel stuck and miserable watching their son struggle with his fears.

Worries and Fears in Early Childhood

All children have worries and fears, as we mentioned earlier. However, the types of fears change as your child develops, so it's important to consider what these look like in early childhood (Muris et al. 2000). To help understand the difference between developmentally normal fears and fears that reflect clinical problems, researchers have studied the ages at which specific types of fears are most likely to occur. We describe common early childhood fears below.

During infancy and toddlerhood, children often fear loud noises, strangers, new places, and heights. They may express their fears by seeking the comfort of parents, or they may limit their exploration and play when they're feeling anxious. As children enter the preschool years, they tend to fear being alone or without parents and/or fear the dark, animals, and imaginary creatures. At this age, separation fears and nighttime fears are fairly common. These fears may give rise to reluctance to be dropped off at day care or preschool as well as resistance at bedtime. By the time children are school-age, their social needs and sensibilities have grown more sophisticated. Thus, they may begin to express fears of negative evaluation by others. They may also experience performance fears or fears of illness or bodily injury, supernatural phenomena (such as ghosts), or natural disasters. Temporary anxieties are part of normal development. Therefore, within these developmental windows the types of fears listed are expected and less likely to indicate a problem, particularly if they're associated with minor avoidance or discomfort and they pass over time.

How Do You Know It's a Problem?

Anxiety falls along a continuum from less to more and is experienced by all children (and adults) to varying degrees on a regular basis. However, even if the content of the fear—for example, fear of strangers or fear of the dark—is in line with what you might expect for a given age, it's still possible that your child has a larger problem if the fear is more extreme, causes significant distress and/or avoidance, and lasts beyond its developmental window. Your child may feel anxious—or worry that bad or frightening things might or could happen in the future—in the absence of any real stressors. He might *ruminate* about things—that is, think about things over and over—so that his worries get worse. He may experience anxiety that seems out of proportion to actual situations. If anxiety occurs out of context or if your child perceives it as very intense or dangerous in and of itself, her mind might kick in with worries *about* her worry—that is, she may grow concerned that she worries too much, or she may wonder what's wrong with her when she can't stop feeling anxious. She might worry that there's something wrong with her *because* she can't stop worrying or feeling anxious. This can get in the way of everyday functioning and become a real problem for your child and your family. If this is the case for you and your child, your child may benefit from treatment, so you may want to consider getting professional help.

How Can ACT Help?

Even when your child's fears and anxieties are what you might expect given his age, it can still be a challenge to know what to do and, more importantly, to do what is needed to support your child. Very often you can get sucked into a pattern of handling your child's fears that is unhelpful. This type of pattern is called *accommodation,* and it tends to reinforce avoidance of feared situations. In the sections below, we'll discuss triggers that may contribute to accommodation of some typical early childhood anxieties and provide ACT tools for helping you to develop more effective strategies. You can use these strategies to respond to your child's anxiety in an empathic and firm way that will help her learn to accept rather than avoid. You'll find that even though the content of the fears may differ, the general principles for how to address them are the same: to model and encourage approach, willingness, and accep-tance in the service of your child's chosen values.

Separation Anxiety

Your child, like many children, may experience separation anxiety, especially when he begins to attend day care or preschool. He may grow tearful, cling to and plead with you, and sometimes grow stubborn and angry about being separated from you. He may seek reassurance about being separated. Again, this is very common for children of this age. If your child is school-age, her separation anxiety may manifest as resistance to going to school, excessive checking or reassurance about your whereabouts, or numerous physical com-plaints (like headaches or stomachaches) at school. Separation anxiety may come and go with stressors and transitions. The vast majority of children tend to recover quite quickly from their anxiety. For others, their anxiety can become so severe that they have significant difficulty even being in a different room from their parents. Anxiety at this level of intensity may also signal other worries—for example, concern that something terrible might befall a parent during the separation. Children who've experienced some sort of trauma might struggle in this way as well.

If your child demonstrates separation anxiety, strategies you use may help to facilitate her adjustment—or to hinder it. Consider the function of your parenting behavior—that is, why you're doing what you're doing (see chapter 4)—to help determine whether it supports your child or inadvertently reinforces her fear. For example, does your behavior communicate to your child that things will be okay when you leave, or does it suggest that she cannot go it alone? A warm but quick and firm good-bye at drop-off time may suggest the former, while lingering and soothing your child may speak volumes about the classroom being a potentially scary place. In addition, to best support your child in developing her independence, it's also important to explore the *why* of her behavior. If you can figure out what contributes to your child's resistance to separating from you, you can help her overcome this resistance. The way to start thinking about each of these tasks is to identify the triggers and setting events for your child's separation fears.

Triggers and Setting Events

It's probably difficult for you to watch your child feel anxious or fearful. You, like most parents, likely feel that you should be able to soothe your child and make the fears go away. However, as we've mentioned here and in previous chapters, trying to make an emotion go away is usually unhelpful and may sometimes have the paradoxical effect of making things worse. For example, picture your child's separation anxiety as a baby tiger that growls when it's hungry. If you or your child feed the tiger, the growling may stop for a while, but the tiger grows and grows. And after a time, it growls again when it's hungry, and this time, it's larger and louder. Childhood fears can be like that too: the more you try or your child tries to make them go away, the more persistent and intense they can become. The next exercise will help you focus on the triggers and consequences, as well as the functions, of your own and your child's behaviors.

EXERCISE: The Why and What For of Anxiety and Avoidance

Think about a time that your child resisted separating from you, perhaps the first day at a new camp or school. Imagine it now in as much detail as possible.

1. Identify the context: Where are you and your child? What is going on around you when your child begins to resist your leaving?

2. Identify antecedents for your child: Write down how your child behaved in the moments just before the separation from you: What was he doing? What did his face and posture look like? What was he saying?

3. Identify your behavior: How do you respond? What do you do? Write it down in as much detail as possible.

4. Identify the consequences for your child: What happens to your child's behavior? Now write down the short-term consequences: What happens for your child in this situation in the short run?

5. Identify the consequences for you: Immediately after you use this tactic, what happens to your thoughts and feelings? Do they change? Would you describe yourself as feeling better or worse?

6. Consider longer-term consequences: What do you think will happen the next time you have to separate from your child?

What did you learn from the exercise? Did you notice how your thoughts and feelings influenced what you chose to do in response to your child's anxiety? Were the things you chose to do helpful? What about in the long run? If you're like many parents, you might have felt uncomfortable with encouraging your child to face her fears—and yet sometimes that's exactly what is needed.

Behavioral techniques that have been shown to work well to address child anxiety nearly all involve some form of *exposure*—that is, willingly facing fears. Yet this can feel very distressing for you as a parent. In our clinical experience, we have repeatedly seen that it's harder for parents to set limits around their child's anxiety and avoidance than with anger and argumentative behaviors. Very likely this is related to the "meanings" your child's anxiety may have for you. Try the following exercise to explore the meanings you may give to your child's separation fears.

EXERCISE: Mindful Awareness of My Child's Anxiety

1. Recall a specific situation when your child did not want to separate from you.

2. Picture the situation in as much detail as possible: Where are you? How is your child behaving? What does each of you look like? What do each of you say? Become present to this experience of separation.

3. Now allow your awareness to turn inward—be present to the thoughts, feelings, and bodily sensations that you have in that moment. Some parents have thoughts like *If I leave him here, he might cry until he makes himself sick* or *I have to help him calm down before I go.* Many parents feel guilty and embarrassed that their children are making a scene. Write about the thoughts, feelings, and bodily sensations you have as you try to separate from your child.

4. What happens next? What are the consequences, both in the short run and in the long run?

5. Reflect on these questions: If you hover over your child and watch her every move and coach her to depend on you, will she ever learn to be on her own? If you give in to your feelings of embarrassment and stay to comfort your child, will you be able to do what you need to do (for example, make it to work on time)? If you're concerned about making your child feel abandoned, do you neglect to help him feel powerful by encouraging independence?

What was it like to consider these questions? What thoughts and feelings showed up for you as you worked through them? If you're like many parents, you may attribute many things to your child's expressed anxiety: for example, that it may harm him or that he cannot handle it. These meanings may, in turn, contribute to how you choose to handle separation situations. If you choose to stick around and "help" your child, while that may give him some relief, this may not be the most helpful strategy in the long run. Below we discuss some tools to help you and your child manage separation situations.

Parenting Strategy: Useful Separation Skills

Separation fears call for "separation skills"—helpful things that you can do in supporting your child when she feels fearful about leaving you. Now that you've completed the exercise above, you know what shows up for you when your child expresses separation fear. Even as you experience those thoughts and feelings, are you willing to take concrete action to support your child? If so, consider using the separation skills below:

- Acknowledge your child's experience of fear and empathize with him. Resist soothing or attempting to minimize his fear. Don't try to talk him out of his fear.

- If your child is a preschooler, have a morning "good-bye routine." This may begin at home or on the way to school or day care. Describe how the routine will go in specific, concrete detail and then stick to that routine.

- When you leave your child, kneel down and look into her eyes; let her know that you love her. Acknowledge and empathize with her anxiety, tell her she'll be okay and to have a good day, then leave.

- Sometimes it's helpful to ask your child's teacher for support in advance. The teacher may assist with holding your child as you exit, making a space in the classroom for him to cry or be anxious, then helping him engage in his favorite classroom activity.

- If your school-age child drags her feet or resists going to school, it may be helpful to set up a token system (see chapter 8) to support more timely morning preparation.

- In concert with the token system, set limits on school-refusal behavior. Providing mild punishing consequences, such as loss of privileges, in addition to rewards, can sometimes help facilitate school attendance.

- If your child whines or seeks excessive reassurance when you separate, use planned ignoring (see chapter 6) to help set limits on those behaviors.

Remember these four steps to help your child to be brave when separating from you:

1. Empathize without soothing.

2. Praise your child for his courage.

3. Ignore whining, reassurance seeking, and protests.

4. Quickly and firmly leave or drop your child off.

Using these four steps well will help support your child in facing his fears. Try the next exercise to think through more specifically how and when you might use them.

EXERCISE: Using the Four Steps to Encourage Bravery

1. In your parenting journal, write down specific examples of ways that you can practice each of the four steps listed above. (For example, to empathize without soothing you might say to your crying child, "It's okay to feel scared sometimes, and it's okay to cry. I get scared too. I even worry about leaving you, just like you worry about it. But sometimes we do things even when we're scared because we need to for something important. I know that you can walk into your classroom all by yourself. And I will see you later.")

2. Think about how you and your child handle separations now. List the ways in which your current separation experience differs from what you wrote above. This will help you think about how you need to get from where you are now to where you want to be. You'll probably note some strengths in what you currently do, and you'll also note some things that need work.

3. As you consider these changes, let your awareness gently focus on what thoughts and feelings show up for you. Take a few minutes to write those down and to reflect on your list. You might notice that some changes seem easier than others—and that your mind chatters about how other changes will be hard. Write down barriers to change. (For example, you might be having the thought *I can't just let her cry because it kills me to hear it.* This thought could occur as a barrier to ignoring.) Consider all four steps: what barriers might you encounter as you carry out those steps?

4. Focus on those barriers and practice willingness. Brainstorm how you might be less judgmental and more accepting of your child and yourself. Write down how you think this willingness could change the way that you interact with those barriers.

5. Now take a few deep breaths and imagine putting the barriers on clouds and watching them float on by before you follow the four steps.

To summarize, many young children experience separation anxiety. In fact, it's a normal developmental transition. It's important to understand what you as a parent might do to help your child transition out of her separation anxieties. As you have discovered, your thoughts and feelings may play a role in the parenting strategies you choose. However, using ACT-based skills can help you support brave behaviors—like separating from you when starting school—in your child. Next, we'll talk about a different area of early childhood fears: feeling anxious about social situations.

Social Anxiety

Children as young as those in preschool may show hesitancy or discomfort in social situations. It's often difficult for younger children to express social fears, due to their emerging skills in understanding and talking about their feelings. Social fears may be reflected in reluctance to play with other children, or (in large versus small groups of children) a tendency to stand on the sidelines and observe rather than engage in social activities, or as limited conversations with either children or adults. Sometimes young children also cling to parents when they feel socially anxious. In older children, symptoms appear much the same, although school-age youngsters may be better able to express their concerns. The central feature of social anxiety, whether mild or severe, involves fear of embarrassment and/or scrutiny by others. This type of fear can spread across situations or be specific to one situation such as performance, public speaking, or large-group play. We've often seen and heard about very bright kids who won't open their mouths in class, even when they know the answer, for fear of looking silly or being laughed at by peers.

Triggers and Setting Events

If your child demonstrates social anxiety, it's often helpful to determine specifically what types of situations—or interactions with specific people— are most problematic. It's also important to determine when your child feels socially comfortable and competent. If you're able to determine what situations trigger your child's social anxiety, it will help you gain a detailed understanding of a hierarchy of situations that your child is likely to avoid—this is what we call an *anxiety hierarchy*. This is a "ladder," with small fears at the bottom rung, moderate fears in the middle, and the most daunting fears at the top. We use this tool to help children face their fears in small, measured doses. The anxiety hierarchy that you develop can be used to help your child experience (or approach) these feared situations in baby steps. In doing so, you will help her face her fears at a pace that is likely to keep her moving forward in easily mastered steps without feeling overwhelmed. Here are a few things to consider as you begin to build an anxiety hierarchy:

- Is your child more anxious one on one, in small groups, or in large groups?

- Is your child more anxious with family members or strangers? Is your child more anxious with children who are his same age, younger, or older, or is he more anxious with adults?

- In what setting is your child more anxious—school, playground, mall, supermarket, playdates, school cafeteria, bus, or other situations?

- During what types of activities is your child more or less anxious—structured games versus unstructured play, social events like parties versus going to the movies with friends or acquaintances?

Try the exercise below to make an anxiety hierarchy for your own child. Consider the questions above as you work on this.

EXERCISE: Your Child's Anxiety Hierarchy

1. Imagine a ladder. If it would be helpful, draw one in your parenting journal. Each step of the ladder should represent a fear that your child has. Each step corresponds to a specific thing or event (which can include thoughts and feelings as well as external events like being on stage). The bottom step should represent something that your child reacts to mildly— with a little distress or only minor avoidance. The next step should be a little more distressing, and the top step should be the thing or event that your child fears the most. Write these down.

2. Look at the ladder and notice—just notice—what thoughts and feelings you have about each step. Write them in your journal. Once you have

a list of situations, remember that the list can change over time and with your child's experience. For example, if your child is tired or feeling vulnerable for other reasons, even small steps on the ladder can seem insurmountable. Similarly it's important not to push your child too far, too fast. Doing so can create even more resistance to social participation. Thus, it can be very helpful to collaborate with your child on making the hierarchy and deciding where to start. Once your child and you collaboratively decide on which step to try, it's essential to help your child stay in that situation until his anxiety subsides. This can help your child notice that fear, like any other emotion, can come and go. It can also help him understand that fears don't always "come true": for example, just because a child fears that peers will taunt or make fun of him, that doesn't mean it will happen; if it does happen, it doesn't mean that it will be as "bad" as a child thinks it might. Finally, it may help your child experience a social situation differently than he might have before. When your child actively chooses to face his fear willingly rather than feeling as if he's "white knuckling" through anxiety-provoking situations, it can make social situations feel less threatening.

Parenting Strategy: Useful Skills for Social Anxiety

We mentioned earlier that children often learn directly, by their own experience. However, they also learn indirectly, through watching others like parents, caregivers, teachers, and friends and through thoughts or maxims that adults might give a voice to, such as "Big dogs are scary." To give you an example of indirect learning, consider the following: Because a child experiences social anxiety doesn't mean she's suffered embarrassment or rejection at the hands of friends. Just because she may not have directly experienced traumatic social events doesn't mean that her anxieties are any less real. This is important to understand, because sometimes when you hear your child express anxiety, you may feel inclined to reinterpret your child's experience. You may, for example, dismiss your child's anxiety as unreasonable or "not that bad." Even though your child may not have had a direct learning experience that has contributed to her worries, her experience is *real* to her.

There's a flip side to this sort of indirect learning. Because your child also learns through observing others, you as a parent can be a helpful model in demonstrating how to behave in social situations and how to handle such interactions when they don't go as well as you might like. In this section, we'll introduce *modeling*, which means teaching your child by demonstrating a particular action or coping response yourself. It's an indirect method of teaching that, when harnessed well, can be a useful strategy to help your child learn to approach and not avoid feared situations. To begin, try the following exercise to identify how someone you think is highly socially skilled and resilient might handle potentially embarrassing social situations.

EXERCISE: Letting It Roll Like Water off Your Back

1. Think of an adult you know who usually lets things go easily, in a very "cool" way. Imagine him or her in an embarrassing situation. Picture the situation that you choose in as much detail as possible. You might, for example, imagine this person dealing with their child throwing a tantrum in a crowded restaurant. To make it even worse, imagine that the waiter has stated that if the parent cannot control the child, the family will have to leave.

2. What is the person doing? What is he or she saying? What about his or her facial expression? How are other people responding?

3. Consider the ways in which your current behavior in embarrassing situations is similar to and different from this person's behavior. In your parenting journal, write down how you feel about your behavior.

4. Brainstorm ways that you might model for your child similar skills for "letting fears roll off her back" and support him in carrying them out. Consider the following example to help you get started.

❧ *Are They Laughing at Me?*

Bethy, who was seven, sat on a bench at the playground with her mother, Kate. There were a few other children nearby, who appeared close in age to Bethy, but she didn't attempt to join in their play. Instead she gazed at them wistfully. Kate asked, "Bethy, why don't you go play with those kids?" "I'm scared to, Mom. I think they're laughing at me." The children were indeed laughing and occasionally glanced in Bethy's direction. "Hmmm," said Kate. "What do you think would be more fun: sitting on this bench or maybe making some new friends to play with?" "I don't know," said Bethy. "This is sort of boring, but what if those girls aren't nice?" "Hmmm," said Kate again, "I understand. That's a tough choice, isn't it?" "Yeah," said Bethy. Kate noticed a small group of women sitting on another bench, chatting and laughing. "You know, Bethy, I like to make friends too, but sometimes I get scared about going to meet new people. I even feel nervous in my body—my chest feels tight, and I get butterflies in my tummy. Sometimes I worry that people won't like me, or that they'll laugh at me because I might accidentally do something silly. Do you ever feel that way?" "Yeah!" said Bethy. "It doesn't feel good." "I know!" said Kate. "I feel a little like that now, but you know what? I want to go make some new friends, and I'm going to go say hello to those ladies, even though I'm feeling nervous and thinking 'Maybe they are laughing at me.' Here I go! Will you watch and see how I do?" "Okay!" said Bethy.

Bethy saw he group of women stop talking as her mother approached, and then begin to smile and shake her hand. As Bethy watched, some of the women turned their gaze toward her. "That's my daughter, Bethy," she heard her mother say. "Would you like to meet her?" "Sure!" said one of the moms. A few of the other kids had wandered over and were looking at Bethy expectantly. Kate looked over at Bethy and smiled. The next step was up to her.

In the story above, Kate modeled some very important tools for helping her child cope with social anxiety. Specifically she empathized with her daughter through expressing her understanding and sharing her own vulnerability to experiencing anxiety-related thoughts, feelings, and physical sensations. She discussed the situation as a choice with her daughter, which helps children to see that there are more options than simple avoidance of feared situations. Finally, she modeled acceptance and willingness to experience her own anxiety and carry it with her as she engaged in a valued action: introducing herself to some potential new friends. It's equally important to notice what Kate did *not* do in this situation. First, she did not dismiss or attempt to minimize her daughter's fearfulness. Second, she did not coerce or force her daughter to approach the other children. Third, Kate was willing to accept whatever outcome her daughter chose, regardless of whether Bethy chose to approach the girls or their mothers or whether she chose to sit on the bench. This last piece is quite important, because it communicates to your child that she is capable of making her own decisions and experiencing the consequences—whether they are positive ones or anxiety-provoking ones. In short, this encourages independence and mastery of feared situations.

Other Common Early Childhood Fears

So far, we've discussed two types of childhood fears that are fairly common. Your child may experience many other fears as well. We'll discuss a few more typical fears below, and in each exercise we'll suggest some ACT-consistent strategies that will help both you and your child to cope effectively with these fears.

Fear of Animals

Fears about animals, such as fear of strange dogs, typically develop in early childhood. Just to make it clear: a child with a spider "fear" may say she hates spiders, scream when she sees one, and ask someone to get rid of it for her, but then continue on with her day. A child with spider "phobia" may not be able even to look at a spider picture book, may avoid rooms in the house where spiders have been known to reside, and may refuse to play in the backyard because of the chance of a spider encounter.

Does it matter if your child is afraid of spiders? It depends. If her fear of spiders gets in the way of her doing things that are important to her, then the answer is yes. If not, then stick with the principle "if it ain't broke, don't fix it." If there's a problem, you'll want your child to get some distance from her fears. To help your child detach somewhat from her fearful thoughts and experiences about animals or insects, try the exercise below.

EXERCISE: I Never Saw That Before!

1. Play a noticing game with your child. Have your child take a few deep breaths, then tell him to look for the smallest thing that he can find in the room (maybe a dot on the wall or a freckle on his skin). Tell him to pretend he is a scientist and that his job is to describe what he notices as best he can. You can suggest that he talk about its color, shape, size, edges, texture, and so on. Praise him for telling you so many details!

2. Next, have him talk about an animal that scares him. Tell him to describe what it looks like or maybe even draw a picture of it. Or, if this is a specific animal that you can photograph, you could take a picture and use that as you do this exercise. Ask him what the animal in the photo looks like.

3. Encourage him to give as many details as he can notice about the animal. Talk and enthuse about this—especially discuss if he sees something that he never noticed before.

4. Use this opportunity to talk to your child about slowing down, paying attention without judging, and accepting the fear while still doing something fun (looking for new details about the animal like a scientist).

Bedtime Fears

Most parents, at some point during early childhood, help their children through fears at bedtime. These fears can be due to "monsters in the closet," or the dark, or being alone. All families are different. With very young children, some parents allow their children to sleep in the parent bed, or they lie down with their children to help them fall asleep. Other families value independence and have strict routines that culminate in children falling asleep in their own beds without assistance. Those are decisions that you, as a parent, must make for your family.

One issue to consider is that almost all children, at some point, will need to be able to fall asleep, on their own, in their own beds. Sometimes nighttime fears can get in your child's way to mastering this developmental milestone. Here are some questions that may be useful to you as you decide whether your child's bedtime fears are an issue:

- Can your child fall asleep in her own bed? Does she do this?

- Do you have a bedtime routine? Does your child show resistance or distress at bedtime if this routine isn't followed?

- Does your child need excessive reassurance from you at bedtime? Does this process of giving reassurance take a great deal of time?

Do any of these issues interfere with your child's getting enough sleep or with her ability to fall asleep on her own? If the answer is yes, consider taking a more proactive approach to help your child establish a consistent bedtime routine and learn coping skills for bedtime fears. The following exercises will help you brainstorm ways to model skills for coping with these fears.

EXERCISE: The Bedtime Routine

Because it's important that anxious children have a set routine, the first step for coping with bedtime fears involves making bedtime more scheduled and predictable. Take some time now to establish a bedtime routine for your child. In your journal, write down your plan in as much detail as possible, keeping the following in mind:

1. Think about what time your child needs to be in bed so that she can have a good night's sleep. Write down a time and a window around it that's acceptable (for example, 7:30 to 8 p.m.).

2. Think about your child's daily activities. Consider the time in the few hours before you want her to go to bed. Schedule physical activities, but make sure that she has some downtime for a while before she has to go to bed. Write down a few activities that you know tire your child out. Then write down the time at which you'll cut off that kind of activity for the night.

3. Make quiet time, like a story hour, an expected nightly activity. Write down how much downtime your child will have before actually going to sleep, and write what some of these downtime activities might be.

4. Hungry and thirsty children do not sleep well, but having sugar or caffeine (or even a lot of water) shortly before bedtime can be a problem. Experiment with your child to see when eating and drinking should be stopped for the night. Write down your thoughts about the last time food and drink will be allowed for the night.

5. Decide now, ahead of time, what your child will need to do before bed—for example, consider whether you want her to bathe or shower at night or in the morning, and decide about the order of brushing teeth and putting on pajamas. When and how to put away toys may be an important part of this plan as well.

6. Discuss these details with your child. Making a chart that outlines each step helps your child know what to do.

7. Perhaps the most important part of the routine is the actual saying "good night" and separating until the morning. Plan this well ahead of time too. Think about whether you are comfortable reading and singing to

your child while she lies in bed or whether you prefer to do such things prior to going into her room. Consider whether you will tuck her in, whether you'll stay until she's asleep or require her to go to sleep without you in the room, whether her door will stay open, and what the rule will be about getting up. Write these things down—both for yourself and to share with your child.

8. Discuss all of these with your child before bedtime, and repeat them often. You could even practice with your child during the day.

Your being firm and consistent in following this plan will likely make bedtime less scary and make going to bed more pleasant for both you and your child. Over time you can start to change things a bit or shift the routine in order to see how your child reacts and to help him deal with anxiety about change. These are great opportunities to encourage bravery, but at the same time, these changes should be small and gradual. As an example, think of starting your new bedtime routine by lying down next to your child until he goes to sleep for several nights but gradually moving to the floor, then closer and closer to the door before eventually not being in the room at all.

Even with a great plan, and with consideration for change over time, bedtime can be rough. Many children cry, whine, beg to stay up or to get up, or throw a tantrum to avoid anxiety. This can be hard to deal with—and it can make it harder to follow the routine. You'll need your mindfulness skills to get through some nights. The following exercise shows you how.

EXERCISE: Sticking to the Routine

1. Think about a time that your child's bedtime-related behavior caused you to feel stressed, guilty, or otherwise upset. Maybe your little one cried in her crib or your older child repeatedly asked for a snack. Perhaps your child screamed about monsters.

2. Imagine such an event in as much detail as possible, and see what thoughts and feelings are present for you in that moment. In your journal, write down whatever shows up.

3. Imagine those thoughts and feelings on clouds, and watch them float by. Acknowledge them nonjudgmentally. Remember that you can practice this in the moment with your anxious child.

4. Focus on how important it is that your child get to sleep and learn to sleep without you. Your child needs rest to learn and grow, both physically and emotionally. Being present to the importance of sleep—and of independence—might make the crying a bit more tolerable. Practice this awareness now and in the moments that are difficult around bedtime.

5. Thinking of your own anxiety about your child at bedtime and about this mindful and accepting approach to it, take a minute or two now to plan what you can say to your child to acknowledge her fears and encourage her to sleep. Write down several ideas.

Behavioral Rigidity and Reassurance Seeking

Many anxious children, regardless of the type of fear they experience, can be somewhat rigid. This means that their anxiety threshold for new things, or their tolerance for disruptions in routine or uncertainty, can be a bit lower than that of less anxious children. This is due, in part, to their temperament. Many children who experience fear and anxiety will "require" adults to keep things fairly systematic and predictable. This isn't, in and of itself, a problem, unless it compromises your child's—or your family's—pursuit of meaningful or valued ends. This might happen, for example, if your child throws excessive tantrums when unpredictability creeps into your daily routines. Or perhaps you feel that you're spending an excessive amount of time reassuring your child, or that your child excessively checks on things such as what will happen next, where you'll be, and when you'll return. If you feel that some of these things are issues for your child, try the following exercise to learn how to provide structure for your child without accommodating unreasonable requests for certainty.

EXERCISE: Planning for Difficult Situations

1. Pick an event that's difficult for your child—a situation in which he begs to be comforted or requires that you make changes to help him avoid anxiety.

2. Write down, in as much detail as possible, a routine for that event.

3. Write down the ways in which you think your child might create barriers that interfere with the plan being carried out. Barriers—like needing to

be dropped off for school at a certain corner even though it makes you late, for example—should be detailed.

4. Now write down a plan for how you will handle each of the listed barriers. What will you do? What will you say to him? What will you require that he do, and how will you reinforce his doing it? Don't forget to consider how you're going to approach thoughts and feelings—both yours and your child's.

Now that you have read about a variety of different fears and anxieties that arise in early childhood, you may have noticed some patterns. Young children who feel anxious tend to avoid things they fear. Your role as a parent is to help encourage them to face their fears, especially when fears get in the way of activities or relationships that are important to your child. Sometimes it's hard to do this, especially when you as a parent worry about your child as she experiences anxiety. However, in those moments, you might unwittingly use strategies that are unhelpful to your child. Below are a few tips to help you get through these difficult moments.

Unhelpful Consequences

When your child is afraid of something—whether it's a dog, a spider, being away from you, or peer teasing—she may avoid situations in which those things occur. But something else may happen as well; she may pay attention to only those things that she's afraid of rather than other things that are going on around her. If the focus of her attention is rigid and narrow, this prevents her from having a richer and more detailed experience that could broaden her awareness and learning. Her experience will broaden when she's able to behave more flexibly as she encounters the things she fears. Encouraging this flexibility is your task as a parent of an anxious child, and it's not an easy one.

It can be stressful for you as a parent—as well as for your child—to encourage him to face his fears such as participating in a social occasion, separating from you, or interacting with an animal that frightens him. There may be times when it feels easier to simply allow your child to avoid things and situations that are uncomfortable rather than encouraging his participation. This may be because your child grows stubborn, or tearful and sad, or both, when asked to engage with something he fears.

Sometimes avoidance is a perfectly good response to your child's discomfort. For example, if your child is afraid of a neighbor's dog that does bite, you might actually recommend avoiding that particular dog. However, if avoidance interferes with activities or relationships that your child values—or that you and your family value—that can be a problem. So if your child avoids all dogs in addition to the mean dog that bites, and this avoidance prevents him from enjoying playdates at friends' homes where there are dogs, this could be a problem. In situations like these, consider what's most important to your child and your family. Try the exercise below to explore your child's—and your family's—values as well as how avoidance might facilitate or impede your pursuit of valued directions. We've already talked some in this chapter about the consequences of avoiding anxiety. Here we hope to emphasize that avoidance sometimes works, but it also sometimes gets in the way of your values. See if this is true for you and your child.

EXERCISE: On the Mark?

1. Consider what you most want for your child—what you hope for with respect to your relationship, to her development, to his emotional well-being, and so on. You've written about this before, but go ahead and jot down some ideas now about what you value for your child and your relationship.

2. Imagine those values being described by specific goals. You don't have to write them down, but do fully consider them. What would you be doing, and what would your child be doing, if you were living out these values perfectly and consistently all of the time? Imagine that all of those goals and the perfection of your goal-supporting behaviors are represented by a dart on the bull's-eye of a target.

3. Now consider all of the ways that you've been avoiding anxiety. Think also of all the ways in which you allow your child to avoid anxiety. Maybe you start to feel worried about your child at day care, so you leave work early to check on her. Perhaps you pick him up from school early, so that he doesn't have to be in a crowd of students. Many different parents avoid in many different ways. Write down your avoidant strategies in your journal.

4. Consider your behavior when you're really avoiding a lot. If you could place it on the target, how far would it be from the bull's-eye? Write down if you would be near or far from it, and also write down what thoughts and feelings you have concerning this distance.

5. Take a minute or two to think about ways that you could decrease the distance—to bring yourself closer to your values. Write down your thoughts and feelings about that.

6. Come back to the idea of the bull's-eye every two weeks or once a month to help you see how you're doing at living out your values. You also might try doing this exercise with your child. Ask what she cares about and what she wants, then talk about the behaviors that go along with moving in that direction. Make a target and have your child mark the bull's-eye with you. Even young children do this fairly well, and this activity can give you an opportunity to check in as well as to model willingness, mindfulness, and acceptance.

A Few Words on Coercion

When you consider what you most value, sometimes your own values for your child may conflict with your child's. For example, you might value your child being a social butterfly, being outgoing and friendly and enjoying being surrounded by many friends. However, if your child has a more inhibited temperament, this may be inconsistent with what he wants for himself. Perhaps he prefers a few playdates every few weeks or enjoying a movie with one or two friends rather than more ambitious social events. Thus, it's important to make a space for your child to be himself. Acknowledge your own hopes and dreams, and hold them and accept them in a way that does not coerce your child to behave in ways that conflict with who he is. This is a difficult balance to make and keep, and one that may be a constant struggle for you as a parent. Nonetheless it's one that is hugely worthwhile in the service of supporting your child's willingness to participate in social events (or other feared situations) at his own pace. This will help you work with, instead of against, your child to help him follow his own valued course.

> ### EXERCISE: Understanding the Function of Your Behavior

1. Think of a recent social interaction or similar situation that your child feared. Imagine it in as much detail as possible.

2. Allow your awareness to focus inward. In the moment of that interaction, what are you thinking and feeling? Are you remembering anything? Do you feel anything in your body?

3. Write down in your journal what you do in that moment—and what happens just afterward.

4. Looking at what you just wrote, what do you think the function of your behavior is in this situation? Consider the following to help you answer: Do you force your child to do particular activities, like sports or gymnastics, because that's what children are supposed to do, or because you did, or because you wanted to but never got a chance? Do you encourage your child to go on stage at day care because you think it will help her conquer her worries about other children looking at her in a mean way?

5. Parents do many different things to deal with anxiety, and each of these behaviors can be done for many different reasons. Really think about you and your child. Are you managing your own discomfort in some way or helping your child to live a productive, meaningful life, or is it some combination of both?

6. Write down your thoughts about this and then spend some time noticing, without judgment, your feelings about it.

Your Child Is Not Broken

One theme that we've touched upon throughout this chapter is how very hard it can be for you as a parent to watch your child feeling anxious and fearful. It may also be difficult for you to encourage your child to approach, rather than avoid, things he fears. Doing so, of course, will increase your child's level of anxiety. However, it will also help your child to carve out a bigger, broader, and more spacious world in which to live and to experience life in a rich, accepting way.

Often, providing comfort for your child may be your first defense when your child feels frightened or anxious. And that's perfectly okay in some situations. However, in situations in which your child struggles with a long-standing or intense fear, it may send an unintended message: that your child isn't capable of holding and appreciating her own experience of fear or anxiety. It may also contribute to the idea that anxiety and fear are always bad and must be made to stop in order to have fun or play with friends.

Asking your child with compassion and empathy to face his fears—or modeling "brave" behavior for him—sends a different message: that your child is *not* broken. It sends a message that he is strong, that he can be brave, and that you will help him, in little steps, perhaps, even when it's hard. So although it might feel uncomfortable for you to watch him as he walks bravely into scary situations, he'll need you to go with him and to believe in his strength, even if you're feeling frightened yourself. Try the exercise below to help you make a commitment to standing with your child as he faces his fears.

EXERCISE: Commitment

1. As we've stated several times, all children and parents are sometimes anxious. Perhaps your child is more anxious than some others—that does not have to mean anything. Keeping this in mind, state what you hope your child will do with her life regardless of anxiety.

2. Now think of all of the behaviors that you can do to help her achieve the life that you hope for her, if she chooses it.

3. Write down what you're willing to do for her to ensure that she lives a valued life—that she moves ahead, with or without anxiety. This is your commitment to her—share it with her. Make sure that she knows that moving forward does not mean *not* being afraid. Make sure she knows that your hope is that she gets to choose to act freely rather than simply respond to anxiety and fear.

Summary

In this chapter, we described how to use ACT and effective strategies to help you deal with your child's anxieties and common early childhood fears (including separation, social situations, animal, and bedtime) and excessive rigidity and reassurance seeking. We defined fear as having two parts. These are the psychological experience of fear (including thoughts, bodily sensations, and emotions) and avoidance. We also discussed parenting behaviors that are unhelpful (accommodation) and helpful (encouraging bravery and facing fears) in fostering participation in valued activities. Most of these tools have been introduced in previous chapters, and here we provided a number of opportunities for you to think through how to use them with your child's— and your own—avoidance. In the next chapter, we'll discuss how to use ACT-based skills across many different situations and how to keep on using them consistently when the going gets tough. We'll also talk about self-compassion when you may face additional parenting challenges.

CHAPTER 10

Putting It All Together

Some Final Tools

*And the end of all our exploring will be to arrive where we started
and know the place for the first time.*

T. S. Eliot

In previous chapters, we helped you to touch upon what is most important to you in parenting your child. Despite your passion to pursue these valued ends, you may encounter many bumps in the road. These might include particularly difficult situations, such as when your child misbehaves in public, or novel situations that either you or your child are not prepared for. As you pursue your parenting values, you may face obstacles such as difficulty implementing parenting strategies or dealing with your mind's negative chatter. It's precisely during these times that it's most important not only to hold true to your values but also to act on them.

In this chapter, we'll explore how you can extend the skills you've already learned to more difficult situations and how commitment to following your values will help you maintain a course toward those outcomes that are most important to you for your child. We'll also help you to identify events that may nudge you off course, so that you're better able to parent effectively when the going becomes tougher. It's our hope that we can also show you how to be gentle with yourself as you use these ACT-based skills to navigate the early childhood years.

Living Your Parenting Values

Now that you've made your way through our book, take some time to sit quietly with your thoughts and take stock. We hope that we've given you some tools to help you through both the storms and the joyful moments of early childhood. Take a few minutes to slow down and reflect on your relationship with your child from birth to this moment. Welcome all the thoughts, feelings, memories, and images that may show up for you. Make a space for moments that are peaceful or joyful as well as for those that are painful or difficult. See if you can welcome these as you might welcome friends, then sit with them as long as you can. All of these thoughts, feelings, memories, and images offer something of value for you as you strive to embark on a new course in your relationship with your child. Take a moment to reflect on your willingness to carry what you're thinking and feeling in an accepting way, without struggle, as you strive to parent consistently based on your parenting values. If you notice doubts or concerns, welcome them. If you are visited by hope and a sense of purpose, welcome those feelings as well. All of these thoughts, feelings, memories, and images will come and go as they please. You, as a parent, can choose to make a place for them—or not. Here's an exercise to help you touch upon your wishes and hopes for your child and to help you encounter your thoughts and emotions in this context.

EXERCISE: A Look Back

1. Take about five minutes to think about and complete the following sentence in your journal: My childhood was...

2. Read your statement about your childhood. Notice how it makes you feel and what thoughts it triggers. Notice whether any specific memories show up. Write these reflections in your journal.

3. If there's a specific memory, let yourself get present to that moment—in the here and now. Picture it in as much detail as possible, as if you're watching a movie and could place yourself in the scene: Where are you? What are you doing? What thoughts and feelings do you have? Is anyone with you? If so, are they doing? Write down some key words to describe the event (or events, if there is more than one).

4. Imagine that you can rewind and fast-forward to other life events in your childhood. Go to your earliest memory and to your favorite one, then to one that's difficult to consider. Spend some time with each moment and become present to whatever shows up there.

5. Now answer the following questions in your journal: How do you want your child's life to be the same and/or different from yours? If your child were to complete a similar exercise as an adult, what memories do you hope would be present? What do you hope she will see? What do you want him to picture about his life and his relationship with you?

Handling Mistakes

If you're like most parents, it's easy to follow your values when things are going well and challenges are few. However, it gets harder if you feel as if you've made an error or done something wrong. You may notice that the more effectively you move toward your values, the more intensely you'll experience self-doubt. This is because when you approach the things you hold most dearly, the more vulnerable you are: to give voice to something that you want comes hand in hand with the fear that you will lose that thing.

When you stray from your course, understand that this departure is not an endpoint or failure. Failure is a choice that you and you alone can make. After all, you fail only when you choose to give up and stop trying. Nonetheless, when you feel you've done something wrong, you may experience it as failure. However, this is merely a reminder that you, too, are human. Remember that parenting effectively isn't a task that ends, or a quota that you can fill, or a place at which you can safely arrive. Parenting will last for your whole life. Your choice, very simply, is to turn away from it—or toward it. All parents can be pulled off track by how their children respond as well as by what their minds tell them. What's important here, however, is what you choose to do *after* you drift from your course. Choosing to turn back toward effective parenting can be a difficult decision. What's more, you may not feel it's a "decision," especially when you're engaged in knee-jerk responding, but it is. And here's another place where mindfulness can help you. Try the following exercise to practice your mindfulness skills when you feel that you haven't been an effective parent.

EXERCISE: Making Space for Failure

1. Think of a time when you feel as if you made a parenting mistake—big or small. Picture it now, in as much detail as possible. Allow yourself, in this moment, to get present to what thoughts, feelings, bodily sensations, and memories show up.

2. In your journal, write down key words to describe the feelings related to making a mistake as a parent, and to experiencing that mistake as failure.

3. Look over your notes for step 2. Notice if you want to give up or avoid trying new things with your child because failure feels so bad.

4. Look at the words again and notice your feelings without attempting to avoid or change them—without judging them.

5. Now look again at your notes for step 2. Sometimes when you experience powerful feelings or when you're feeling vulnerable, there's a value hidden there. As you let these feelings linger, can you identify a value or something of great meaning to you? Consider this: if you want to abandon a parenting strategy because it's hard, is there a long-term consequence for your child or for what you hope for your relationship?

6. Allow yourself to think that the possibility of failure is a necessary part of parenting well. Failure is the result of trying to do something for your child. Avoiding the possibility of failure means avoiding the possibility of being an extraordinary parent—and avoiding what you want for your child. As you lightly hold this idea (without evaluating it or arguing with it), consider your willingness to fail in the service of working for your child.

7. Practice willingness now, being open to whatever thoughts and feelings show up.

We live in a culture in which we're taught that failure isn't acceptable. Yet failure is a part of living and parenting well. What we said above bears repeating: avoiding the possibility of failure means avoiding the possibility of being an extraordinary parent—and avoiding what you want for your child. Your practice of willingness—especially in difficult moments when things haven't gone as well as you'd hoped—is essential to moving yourself back on course and acting on your values in the service of working for your child.

Dealing with Life Stressors

You may experience times when it's difficult to act on your parenting values, and these situations have little to do with your child. You may experience other stressors in your life; these may include financial, marital, and work- or health-related issues. If you're going through a particularly difficult time, or your family faces significant challenges, your focus on parenting may fall by the wayside. It's especially during these times that your young child may most need your support and guidance, and yet you may feel at your most compromised. When this occurs, you may feel trapped or oppressed by parenting your child. Or you may "turn off" or find yourself "going through the motions" simply to get through your day and accomplish the many things you need to do. It can be hard to be emotionally present for your child if you're feeling spent and at the end of your rope. Take a few moments to try the following exercise to help you stay present with your child even when things are at their most difficult.

EXERCISE: A Lot Going On Here!

1. Think of a time in your life when things have been chaotic and stressful—when life circumstances have stacked the odds against you. Perhaps you lost your job, or maybe you or your child got sick, or many bad things happened all at once. Picture now whatever the exact problems were—or are—for you.

2. Let yourself think about your interactions with your child at such times. Imagine watching your parenting as if you're watching a movie, scene by scene. Notice that there are many things going on in each scene—and that you have multiple responsibilities to fulfill. Look for moments when you react in a less than ideal way because you are tired, sad, scared, or otherwise distressed—moments when you avoid or don't do the "work" of parenting because it's just too much.

3. Let your awareness turn inward to what you're thinking and feeling. Write in your journal about how parenting feels in such an overwhelming situation. If you have thoughts or feelings about those feelings, write these down too.

4. Next, see if you can notice the feelings in an accepting and mindful way. Examine them—kindly and gently—in new ways: If you were to give those feelings a shape, what would it be? Are the feelings light or heavy? Do they have a color and texture? If so, what color and texture do they have? Sit with your feelings—and their shape, weight, color, and texture, if they have them—knowing that life is sometimes hard, and parenting is often stressful.

5. Take a couple of minutes to return to the stressful scene you named above. Do you notice anything different now, anything that you missed before? Allow yourself to make space for a simple awareness and appreciation of yourself, your life, and your child even in this most difficult of times.

The gift of awareness—and of being truly present to your child—is something that can get lost in the storm and stress of life. Yet it's also something that you can simply reach out and touch whenever you want to or whenever you notice that you're caught up in other things. You have a limitless capacity to be present with your child even when circumstances are more difficult than ever. As you work through difficult times in your own life, see if this is true for you. With time and practice, this way of being—this gentle, compassionate, present-moment awareness—can become something you call upon at will.

What If How You Parent Is Not Enough?

Even if you do everything right, sometimes it isn't enough. This is one of the hardest truths of parenting: that even if you do all the right things, you are not in control of how your child will grow up. Just as you make your own choices, so will your child. And your child's future will ultimately be determined by many things, not the least of which is your parenting. It can be difficult to acknowledge and appreciate your lack of control as a parent. It can also be confusing to hold the knowledge that, while your influence is only one of many factors that shape your child's future, it's still an important one that merits a great deal of care and attention. This awareness of your limitations as a parent is particularly important—as well as particularly difficult—in early childhood.

When you parent to control or prevent a feared negative outcome, your action—or inaction—can get in the way of effectively using the parenting strategies we've presented in previous chapters. It can also knock you off a valued course, even though it may seem that you're headed in the right direction. In your parenting journal, try the following exercise to see if you can identify situations in which you might be responding to your fear or unease about a potential outcome rather than being mindfully present and proactive with your child. Even though you can't control outcomes for your child, you can parent unconditionally with all your heart.

EXERCISE: Unconditional Parenting

1. Think now of a particular behavior that you want your child to stop, such as whining, hitting, lying, or refusing to go to sleep. Pick something that really bothers you, something that makes you concerned about your child's well-being or healthy development.

2. Write down specific ways in which you can help your child to quit that behavior—ways that you can set up her environment so that she doesn't need to whine or consequences that you can use that would make her less likely to refuse to go to bed. You can, for example, ignore whining and only respond to your child when she uses her "big girl voice," or you can create a nighttime routine that encourages going to bed. Be specific.

3. Now imagine a situation in which you're doing those behaviors that you wrote about in step 2—picture yourself parenting perfectly—and imagine your child "not playing along." For example, she's whining, and her whining is getting louder. Or he's crying outside his bedroom, clinging to you.

4. Let your awareness turn inward: look for anger, frustration, fear, disappointment, and guilt and also for understanding, compassion, love, and appreciation. Write down whatever thoughts, feelings, memories, and bodily sensations are there in that moment.

5. Hold all of those feelings gently, as if they were delicate glass ornaments. Imagine doing the next right thing to put you back on course. What might you do now? Think about what the next step is and write it down.

6. Remember that you can choose—no matter how you feel in the moment, no matter how your child responds—to parent based on what you want for your child and for your relationship with her. And when you find yourself parenting to stop feeling bad, notice that—and then get back on course again.

When Things Don't Go As Planned

Sometimes things simply don't go as planned. When this happens, it's important to understand that nobody is perfect. Sometimes when parents tell us that tried-and-true strategies "don't work," it's because those strategies weren't implemented well. Sometimes their parenting lacked consistency; at other times, they may have applied a rule rigidly and insensitively or at the wrong time. Thus, it's important for you as a parent to be able to mindfully walk back through difficult situations in which things might not have gone the way you planned. In order to figure out what went wrong, objectively revisit the scene in order to check out what worked—and what didn't—in your use of parenting strategies. Certainly many external situational things can trigger ineffective parenting. However, your own thoughts and feelings can also often serve as triggers.

The table below lists some common mistakes parents often make when using the parenting strategies we've taught you as well as a few common psychological triggers—thoughts or feelings—for them. This list is by no means exhaustive, and your psychological triggers may not be the same as these. However, these are fairly commonly reported by parents in our workshops and in individual parent training.

Common Mistakes in Using Parenting Strategies	Possible Psychological Triggers
Giving a direction but failing to ensure that your child follows through	Irritation; thoughts that your child should have listened in the first place; not being present or being distracted by other things
Giving in to your child after you've set a limit	Embarrassment if your child escalates his behavior, especially if you're in public; feelings of being overwhelmed; thoughts that it might be easier to just "give in"; talking yourself out of the need for a limit; muscle tension or stress headache
Using punishment instead of reward to teach appropriate behavior	Feelings of anger or frustration; thoughts that your child "deserves" punishment or that punishment will "teach" your child; feeling that you need to react quickly to misbehavior; not being mindfully present when your child is misbehaving
"Trying" a number of different things instead of dealing with misbehavior in a consistent manner	Thoughts that you've tried a particular strategy before or that, after having tried something a few times, it hasn't worked; feelings of frustration or embarrassment if your child's behavior escalates once a limit has been set

Sometimes when you notice yourself falling into patterns where you're making one or more of these common mistakes, it helps to check out what's going on in your life outside of your parenting. For example, are you experiencing stress in other areas? Is this particular time in your life harder or more challenging than other times? Use the exercise below to explore these questions.

1. Look over the common parenting mistakes in the table above and see if you can remember any times that you fell into one or more of the patterns. Write them down in your journal.

2. Think about your life as though it's a movie that you're watching. See if you can get a sense of it from as far back as you can remember until now. Think about a time when everything was going well for you and for your family. Your lives may have been full of hope and possibility, and you looked forward to more good times. See if you can bring back that moment in your memory as fully as possible. Take a few moments to relish those feelings that you had then as you re-experience them now.

3. Now come back to the time when you fell into a pattern of making common parenting mistakes. How does your life at that time compare to those remembered moments? What are the differences between these times? What are your thoughts and feelings? What about this context seems to contribute to your getting stuck in making parenting mistakes? Take a few minutes to experience those moments and explore how they may differ from other, perhaps more positive or joyful, times in your life.

When you experience stress in other areas of your life, whether this comes from your family, or your job, or your own mental health, it sets the stage for how you choose to parent your child. In the face of multiple stressors, it's easy to fall out of the present moment and ruminate about the past or fret about the future. It's also easy to lapse into using ineffective parenting strategies. Through becoming aware of broader contextual issues that may affect your parenting and your relationship with your child, you'll have a better chance of catching yourself before slipping out of using your ACT parenting strategies.

When to Be Gentle, When to Be Firm

Once you're able to identify triggers of ineffective parenting strategies, it's important not to engage in what we call "reason-giving." In other words, be careful not to use these triggers as excuses—or for rationalizing some of the common mistakes we described above—when you're experiencing significant contextual stressors. For example, you might say, "Oh, I'll just give in this once because I'm feeling so tired" or "He just can't handle school today—he's too anxious, and I have too many other things on my mind to deal with him right now." Minds are pretty good at reason-giving, especially when they're trying to protect you from feeling like you haven't done something as well as you'd have liked. Thus, see if you can notice your own experience of this. When you find yourself engaged in reason-giving, check whether this feels consistent with your parenting values. If it doesn't, see if you can gently make a choice: first, to notice reason-giving for what it is and, second, to firmly turn back to your charted course.

Self-Compassion

All parents make mistakes. When you do, you may beat yourself up. For instance, you might tell yourself that you *never* parent well or that you should just give up because you just can't get it right. When you notice your mind starting up with this sort of talk, remind yourself that you're human. Your mind may tell you that you *are* your mistakes. Notice thoughts like these for what they are: simply thoughts. And what if you were your mistakes? You might stop trying to do things differently, or you might grow so angry or frustrated with yourself that you might give up. If this is consistent with your experience, try the following exercise.

EXERCISE: One Me, a Whole Parent

1. Think of a time when you feel as if you made a mistake—big or small—in your parenting; it can be the same mistake that you wrote about before or a different one. Picture it again as if you're watching a movie. Especially look at yourself—your posture, your facial expressions, the way you're moving, what you're saying; even look at your clothes.

2. Now picture a time—in the same detailed way—when you feel as though you did an extraordinary job as a parent. Look at your posture, your facial expressions, what you did and said—just as you did above.

3. Now take a few moments to recognize that there's a "you" watching yourself in those situations of both failure and success. Consider what you're doing now, where you are. Notice that you exist in both situations—and in this one too.

4. You're the same you, regardless of your "good" or "bad" parenting behavior. There's a bigger you, one that's greater than any collection of your behaviors. You may have different clothes, you may say and do different things, you probably even look different than you did then—and yet there's just one you, a *whole* you, through it all.

5. With this awareness, make a commitment to recommit to your values when you make mistakes or experience slips in your parenting. Write that promise in your journal now.

On Letting Go

Ralph Waldo Emerson once wrote, "Finish each day and be done with it. You have done what you could. Some blunders and absurdities no doubt crept in; forget them as soon as you can. Tomorrow is a new day; begin it well and serenely and with too high a spirit to be encumbered with your old nonsense." While we don't advocate forgetting (since that is a form of avoidance), we do encourage you to forgive yourself for your flaws and mistakes. It's also important to let go of the past, to let the future take care of itself, and to stay in the present moment. Part of parenting mindfully is working to stay in the present with your child rather than in the past or the future. If you're like most parents, you'll find yourself drifting to and fro; sometimes this will have gone on for a while before you catch yourself doing it. Dwelling in the past or worrying about the future colors your view of the present and makes it harder to parent effectively. Thoughts about the past may hook you and drag you out of the present moment. Similarly if you worry about the future, you may expend more energy problem-solving things that may not even happen rather than mindfully, joyfully being with your child. When you're mindful, you're a vessel through which the past and future can briefly alight and then flow through you. Consider the following *jataka*, or parable, which comes from a centuries-old tradition of Zen Buddhist stories. There are many versions of it, and its origins are not clear. We offer our retelling of it here.

❧ The Two Monks at the Riverbank

One lovely fall day, when the sun had not yet given up its warmth, two monks, one young and the other older, were traveling to a distant monastery. There had been a great deal of rain and bad weather recently, which made the path on which they walked quite muddy and difficult to travel. Nonetheless they were grateful for the rays of sunshine warming their backs as they walked on and on.

After a time, the monks grew very weary from their long journey. They were hungry and thirsty, and they wanted more than anything to reach their destination quickly. Yet they had come upon a swollen river, which appeared quite difficult to cross. A young woman, looking annoyed, stood nearby. The younger monk approached her and asked, "Have you tried to cross yet? Can you tell us where there might be a shallow area we might use to get to the other side?" "Does it look like I've tried to cross?" the young woman retorted, then she turned away and ignored him. How rude, he thought. I'll find my own way across. He floundered across the river, at times wandering into deep water and paddling his way out, until he made it to the other bank. As he looked back across at the young woman, she looked furious and desperate to find a better way to cross. Good, thought the young monk. Serves her right.

The older monk, who had been watching the entire scene, simply picked up the woman and carried her across, setting her down on the other side of the river. "Look what you've done," she said. "Now I'm all cold, and wet, and my clothes are ruined!" The older monk gave her a gentle smile and continued on his journey with the younger monk. As they walked, the young monk grew more and more angry. Why did the old monk help that rude woman? She didn't deserve it! He couldn't get thoughts of the woman out of his mind, and he fumed for miles as they walked and walked. He didn't notice the sun on his back or the mud of the path, only his anger at the woman and his frustration with the old monk. Finally, he could contain himself no longer. "Master," he said to the older monk, "why did you carry that woman? She was rude and ungrateful for your help!" "My son," the elder monk replied, "I set her down many miles ago. Why are you still carrying her?"

Try the following exercise to see what you, as a parent, have been carrying all this time.

EXERCISE: What Can You Choose to Put Down?

Take about five minutes now to think about and complete this statement:

In order for me to have a free mind, an open heart, and an unyielding approach to staying in the present moment with my child, I need to let go of ...

The Importance of Self-Care

We've spent a good deal of this book discussing how you as a parent can nurture your child. However, it's of equal importance for you to nurture yourself as a parent. Take a moment to appreciate that your child depends on you. In the entire universe, there's no other person who can be you in this role, in your family. There's likely no one other than you who has a deeper love for your child, who cares more, or who will hurt and grieve more when things go wrong. Take a few moments to allow yourself to be in this space and to notice your feelings about being here.

Given the enormous responsibilities of being a parent—and the joys as well as the sorrows—it's of utmost importance that you take good care of yourself in the service of your values for your child. Part of being competent at any endeavor is knowing your own limits—acknowledging and accepting them. Growth begins in this awareness of your limits, and this awareness enables you to lightly set down any expectations you may have of yourself to be perfect all the time. Give yourself permission to be just as you are: awake and alive, a strong foundation for your child, and a vessel through which thoughts and feelings flow. Just as you may tend to beat yourself up for failures, also remember to celebrate your successes. Use the following exercise to help develop a plan for self-care.

EXERCISE: Self-Care and Asking for Help

1. In your journal, or in a calendar or daily planner, write down any breaks in your schedule, even if they're only for very short periods of time. For example, maybe your child naps every day from 2:00 to 3:00 p.m. Or you have ten minutes after work before you have to start your drive to day care to pick your child up. Look for any gaps in your schedule that are not already filled with structured and hard-to-change activities.

2. Fill in those gaps with structured opportunities to do something for yourself like meditation or exercise—or to give yourself written permission to do nothing!

3. These self-care opportunities should be taken as seriously as everything else in your daily schedule. Don't allow yourself to fill them with something for your child, or something for your partner, or a household chore—unless you really enjoy doing something like dusting!

4. Telling other people that you have scheduled these times is important so they'll know not to ask you for something else during those times. They can also help you stay on track when you feel pulled to do other things. Make a list now in your journal of a few people to tell about your self-care times.

5. Tell those people you listed in step 4 about your plans and tell them—or someone else if it's better for you—that you're going to ask for help when you get overwhelmed. And then ask for help when you need it!

The Journey Continues: Keeping Your Commitment

In chapter 6, we gave you opportunities to make a commitment to your child so that you, as a parent, could help him move in the direction of your hopes and dreams. To keep this commitment, you may find it helpful to touch upon your commitment every so often in an experiential way. Thus, we'll close this book with another opportunity for you to describe your commitment to your child, in a letter. You may choose to show it to your child or not. That's up to you. However, we hope that with this letter, you can express those things that matter most as you nurture your child in a compassionate, effective way through the early childhood years.

EXERCISE: A Letter to Your Child

1. Write a letter to your child—one that you would really give to her when she graduates from high school or when she gets married—one that's meaningful and rich enough to share during one of life's great achievements.

2. Tell your child your hopes for your relationship and what you most want for her.

3. Write about your fears and your vulnerabilities. Tell her what you are worried might stand in the way of your hopes and dreams for her.

4. Finally, tell your child how committed you are to stand for her or to do the right thing for her—no matter how hard it gets.

5. Put this letter in a safe place. One day, perhaps when your child attains a particular milestone or achieves something special, come back to it. You'll know the right moment when it presents itself. Read this letter to yourself and, if you choose, share it with your child.

We hope that this exercise will resonate with your own experience, now that you have finished this book. We also hope that the letter you've written will be a talisman or special symbol that you can hold onto as you grow together with your child.

Summary

In this book, we've described common behavioral challenges that occur in early childhood, when children are two to eight years old. We presented empirically based parent behavior management tactics embedded in an ACT philosophy of parenting. One core tenet of our book is that your experiences as a parent are an important element in how you nurture your child. We proposed that experiential avoidance can interfere with sensitive and effective learning and use of effective parenting strategies. In contrast, we hope that mindful awareness and acceptance will foster parenting that supports your child's development of appropriate behavior and prevents the development of undesirable behavior. We've discussed applications of these skills with acting-out behaviors as well as with worries and fears. Finally, we've touched upon how to keep up these strategies in times when you as a parent may be feeling great vulnerability. We hope that these skills will be useful to you. We wish you well on your parenting journey.

References

Adcock, A., A. Murrell, and D. Woods. 2007. Empirical support for the importance of valuing on psychological well-being. In *Engaging in Life: Values and Valued Action as Catalysts for Change* (J. Plumb, chair). Symposium conducted at the 33rd annual meeting of the Association for Behavior Analysis, San Diego, CA.

Baer, R., G. Smith, J. Hopkins, J. Krietemeyer, and L. Toney. 2006. Using self-report assessment methods to explore facets of mindfulness. *Assessment* 13:27–45.

Blackledge, J., and C. O. Hayes 2006. Using acceptance and commitment therapy in support of parents of children diagnosed with autism. *Child and Family Behavior Therapy* 28:1–18.

Coyne, L. W., A. Burke, and J. B. Freeman. 2008. Cognitive behavioral treatment. In *Handbook of Clinical Psychology*, vol. 2, edited by M. Hersen and A. M. Gross. New York: Wiley & Sons.

Coyne, L. W., C. Low, A. Miller, R. Seifer, and S. Dickstein. 2006. Mothers' empathic understanding of their toddlers: Associations with maternal sensitivity and depression. *Journal of Child and Family Studies* 16:483–97.

Coyne, L. W., and A. Thompson. 2009. The effect of parent locus of control on child internalizing problems as mediated by parental experiential avoidance. Poster presented at the Society for Research in Child Development, Denver, CO.

Dickstein, S., R. Seifer, L. Hayden, M. Schiller, A. Sameroff, G. Keitner, I. Miller, S. Rasmussen, M. Matzko, and K. Magee. 1998. Levels of family assessment: II. Impact of maternal psychopathology on family functioning. *Journal of Family Psychology* 12:23–40.

Dix, T., E. Gershoff, L. Muenier, and P. Miller. 2004. The affective structure of supportive parenting: Depressive symptoms, immediate emotions, and child-oriented motivation. *Developmental Psychology* 40:1212–227.

Fiese, B. 2006. *Family Routines and Rituals.* New Haven, CT: Yale University Press.

Goodlin-Jones, B., and T. Anders. 2004. Sleep disorders. In *Handbook of Infant, Toddler, and Preschool Mental Health Assessment,* edited by R. DelCarmen-Wiggins and A. Carter. New York: Oxford University Press.

Hayes, S. C., K. Strosahl, and K. Wilson. 1999. *Acceptance and Commitment Therapy: An Experiential Approach to Behavior Change.* New York: Guilford.

Hayes, S. [C.], and K. Wilson. 2003. Mindfulness: Method and process. *Clinical Psychology: Science and Practice* 10:161–65.

Hembree-Kigin, T., and C. McNeil. 1995. *Parent–Child Interaction Therapy.* New York: Plenum.

Kazdin, A., and M. Whitley. 2006. Pretreatment social relations, therapeutic alliance, and improvements in parenting practices in parent management training. *Journal of Consulting and Clinical Psychology* 74:346–55.

Larson, R., A. Wiley, and K. Branscomb, eds. 2006. *Family Mealtime as a Context of Development and Socialization: New Directions for Child and Adolescent Development, No. 111.* New York: Jossey-Bass.

Loeber, R., S. Green, B. Lahey, and L. Kalb. 2000. Physical fighting in childhood as a risk factor for later mental health problems. *Journal of the American Academy of Child & Adolescent Psychiatry* 39:421–28.

Luby, J., A. Belden, and E. Spitznagel. 2006. Risk factors for preschool depression: The mediating role of early stressful life events. *Journal of Child Psychology and Psychiatry* 47:1292–298.

Luby, J., C. Mrakotsky, A. Heffelfinger, K. Brown, M. Hessler, and E. Spitznagel. 2003. Modification of *DSM-IV* criteria for depressed preschool children. *American Journal of Psychiatry* 160:1169–172.

Luby, J., C. Mrakotsky, A. Heffelfinger, K. Brown, M. Hessler, and E. Spitznagel. 2004. Characteristics of depressed preschoolers with and without anhedonia: Evidence for a melancholic depressive subtype in young children. *American Journal of Psychiatry* 161:1998–2004.

Muris, P., H. Merckelbach, B. Gadet, and V. Moulaert. 2000. Fear, worries, and scary dreams in 4- to 12-year-old children: Their content, developmental pattern, and origins. *Journal of Clinical Child Psychology* 29:43–52.

Murrell, A., K. G. Wilson, C. LaBorde, C. Drake, and L. Rogers. In press. Relational responding in parents. *Behavior Analyst Today.*

Oppenheim, D., D. Goldsmith, and N. Koren-Karie. 2004. Maternal insightfulness and preschoolers' emotion and behavior problems: Reciprocal influences in a therapeutic preschool program. *Infant Mental Health Journal* 25:352–67.

Patterson, G. 1982. *Coercive Family Process.* Eugene, OR: Castalia Publishing Co.

Pincus, D. B., S. M. Eyberg, and M. L. Choate. 2005. Adapting parent-child interaction therapy for young children with separation anxiety disorder. *Education and Treatment of Children* 28:163–81.

Rogers, F. 2003. *The World According to Mr. Rogers: Important Things to Remember.* New York: Family Communications, Inc.

Roosevelt, Theodore. 1899. The strenuous life. Speech to the Hamilton Club, Chicago, IL.

Shea, S., and L. W. Coyne. 2009. Experiential avoidance, parenting stress, and discipline tactics in low-income, urban families. Manuscript in preparation.

Shea, S. P., M. Sims, and L. W. Coyne. 2007. The role of experiential avoidance in Head Start mothers' emotion regulation and parenting behavior. Poster presented at the conference of the Association for the Advancement of Behavioral and Cognitive Therapy, Philadelphia, PA.

Silvia, K., and L. W. Coyne. 2009. Does mindfulness influence parent–child interactions? Under review.

Singh, N., G. Lancioni, A. Winton, B. Fisher, R. Wahler, K. McAleavey, J. Singh, and M. Sabaawi. 2006. Mindful parenting decreases aggression, noncompliance, and self-injury in children with autism. *Journal of Emotional and Behavioral Disorders* 14:169–77.

Singh, N., G. Lancioni, A. Winton, J. Singh, W. Curtis, R. Wahler, and K. McAleavey. 2007. Mindful parenting decreases aggression and increases social behavior in children with developmental disabilities. *Behavior Modification* 31:749–71.

Wilson, K., and A. Murrell. 2004. Values work in acceptance and commitment therapy: Setting a course for behavioral treatment. In *The New Behavior Therapies: Expanding the Cognitive Behavioral Tradition*, edited by S. Hayes, V. Follette, and M. Linehan. New York: Guilford.

Lisa W. Coyne, Ph.D., is an assistant professor of psychology and director of the Early Childhood Research Clinic at Suffolk University in Boston, MA. She has adapted and used acceptance and commitment therapy (ACT) for families of young children struggling with emotional and behavioral problems, and applies her research to clinical work with young children living in poverty.

Amy R. Murrell, Ph.D., is an assistant professor of psychology at the University of North Texas. She has been actively developing and conducting ACT programs for children and parents since 2000 and is a recognized leader in the field.

Foreword writer **Kelly Wilson, Ph.D.,** is an associate professor of psychology at the University of Mississippi and coauthor of the landmark book, *Acceptance and Commitment Therapy: An Experiential Approach to Behavior Change.*

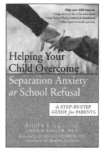